get a grip on

PHILOSOPHY

Get a Grip on PHILOSOPHY

NEIL TURNBULL

Time-Life Books is a division of Time Life Inc.

TIME LIFE INC.
President and CEO: George Artandi

TIME-LIFE BOOKS
President: Stephen R. Frary

TIME-LIFE CUSTOM PUBLISHING

Vice President and Publisher	Terry Newell
Vice President of Sales and Marketing	Neil Levin
Project Manager	Jennie Halfant
Director of Acquisitions	Jennifer Pearce
Director of Design	Christopher M. Register
Director of Special Markets	Liz Ziehl

This book was conceived, designed, and produced by The Ivy Press Limited, 2-3 St. Andrews Place, Lewes, East Sussex BN7 1UP, England

Art Director	Peter Bridgewater
Editorial Director	Sophie Collins
Designer	Angela Neal
Commissioning Editor	Andrew Kirk
Picture Research	Vanessa Fletcher
Illustrations	Andrew Kaulman

First Printing.
Reproduction and printing in Hong Kong by Hong Kong Graphic and Printing Ltd.,

Time-Life is a trademark of Time Warner Inc. U.S.A.

LIBRARY OF CONGRESS CATALOGING-IN-PUBLICATION DATA
Turnbull, Neil
Philosophy / Neil Turnbull.
p. cm.--(Get a grip on ...)
Includes index
ISBN 0-7370-0034-1
1. Philosophy--History. I. Title II. Series
B74.T79 1998
100--dc21 98-29682
CIP

Books produced by Time-Life Custom Publishing are available at a special bulk discount for promotional and premium use. Custom adaptations can also be created to meet your specific marketing goals. Call 1-800-323-5255.

CONTENTS

INTRODUCTION

THE QUESTION OF PHILOSOPHY

philosophy in question

★ Philosophy, in a very simple sense, is all about being curious and asking questions. People have been doing philosophy, as we Westerners understand it, for about 3,000 years. But what sort of questions do philosophers ask? And what are the answers that they get? And what does it have to do with you? Questions, questions. Well, let's start with the basics.

thoughts are more than small change— they're the whole bank!

Wisdom lovers

The meaning of the word philosophy is derived from two ancient Greek words; "philo," meaning "to love" and "sophia," meaning "wisdom." To pursue answers to philosophical questions means to court the love of wisdom, whatever that might be.

HOMO CURIOSUS

is it a crutch?

★ Questioning is a fundamental part of human life. The need to find out more and to look beyond the limitations of our current situation and explore the unknown "beyond" is what makes human life not only both eventful and interesting, but purposeful, too. IT IS THIS BASIC SENSE OF CURIOSITY THAT DRIVES MOST OF OUR DAY-TO-DAY THINKING. Just how of many of our everyday thoughts are questions? It is clearly impossible to be mathematically precise about this matter. Thoughts, unlike money, don't come in small, pocket-sized denominations. Yet, because we are all intimately acquainted with our own thoughts most of us are familiar with the kinds of thoughts that we have. A moment's thought should tell us that most of our lives are spent thinking and that SOME OF OUR CLEAREST THOUGHTS EMERGE FROM A QUESTIONING ATTITUDE TOWARD OURSELVES AND THE WORLD.

SEX AND SHOPPING

* The day-to-day questions that typically occupy us are SO UNEXCEPTIONAL that they usually pass by unnoticed. Our awareness of our own basic underlying curiosity has long since been ousted from our minds by more pressing matters like shopping or sex or, in some instances, both. However, if we stop for a moment we may be startled to realize just what questioning creatures we are. For example, in a typical day we might ask ourselves: "What time is it?" or, "Should I visit my mother soon?" or, "Am I sure I want to visit my mother?" The list of questions occupying the thoughts of the typical person in the street is endless.

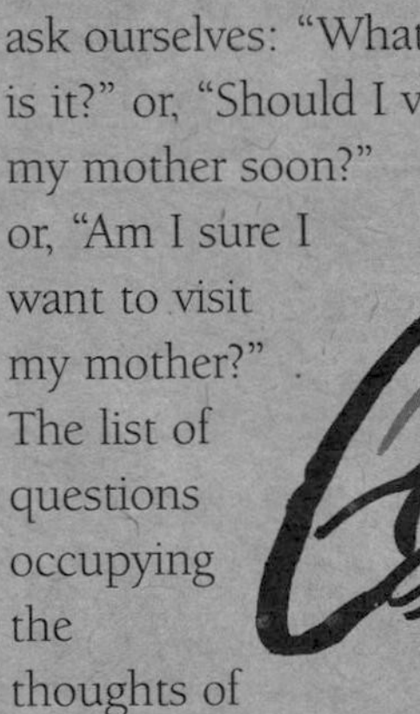

"What time is it?"

KEY WORDS

CURIOSITY: a basic human need to know more about themselves and their surroundings

QUESTIONS: ideas that guide our basic curiosity toward answers

Pandora's box

Although, according to mythology, it was Pandora's curiosity that unleashed all the malignant ills of the world, it is now widely agreed that there can be no human progress without a questioning attitude toward the world. The Swiss psychologist Jean Piaget argued that all our mature adult knowledge about the world is founded on a basic curiosity about our surroundings; therefore without curiosity humans would remain in a state of ignorance.

DIFFERENT TYPES OF QUESTIONS

left my watch at home pal

Before we go any further, it must be said that there are questions and there are, well, questions. The reason for this difference in emphasis is a simple one in that the questions that tend to preoccupy us are obviously not all of the same type. The idea that some questions are much bigger than others is a classificatory scheme that we have all imbibed with our mothers' milk. Some questions claim to be important and significant, while others seem of no real consequence at all.

that was not a worthy question

KEY WORDS

BIG QUESTIONS: questions that because of their scale or scope require unusual ways of thinking to answer them

LITTLE QUESTIONS: conventional questions that can be answered easily by using common-sense criteria

ECONOMICS VS. GUINEA PIGS

* We can define the big questions as those questions that, because they are more costly in terms of time, money, or effort to answer, offer us potentially greater rewards when answers to them are found. For example, the question, "How should the government control inflation?" is clearly a much bigger question than, "How should I control my pet guinea pig?"
* I am not suggesting that we should ALL WORRY ABOUT INFLATION AND NEGLECT OUR PET GUINEA PIGS. The point that I am trying to make is this. Any conceivable answer to the question of how

a **modern economy** ought to be managed will be more complex than any answer to a question concerning pet discipline. Therefore much more time and effort will be required to answer the former question than the latter.

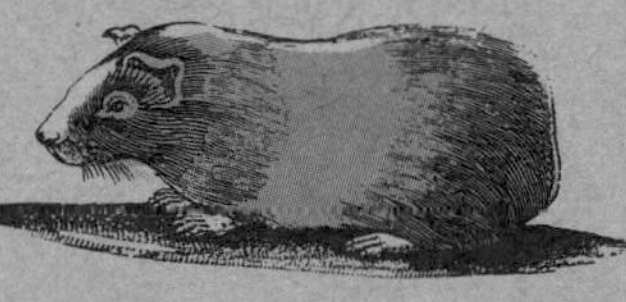

look after your pet guinea pig and let inflation worry about itself

WHO CAN ANSWER THE BIG QUESTIONS?

* In the current **market for questions**, questions about pet control can only be found in the cheap shops, alongside questions about the IDEAL CHIPPED POTATO OR DO-IT-YOURSELF CRAZY PAVING. They are the **ten-a-penny questions** of the modern world and so answers to them are not in great demand.

* Joking aside, there is an important point here. *Because most of the big questions of life are so costly to answer, when we need answers to them, we usually defer to those who have the resources to find those answers.*

* It is a **'lack of information'** that prevents most people from being able to answer many contemporary big questions. In fact, for an increasing number of people, the 'size' of a question is synonymous with its 'information content'. *The bigger the question, the more intensive is the search for the relevant information required to answer it.* This insight gives us another more important way of classifying questions.

The big questions

For many of the big questions facing the world today, there seems to be no agreement as to how they should be answered. This means that big questions are often the source of bitter disputes between different powerful groups.

what are the really big questions?

KEY WORDS

TECHNICAL QUESTIONS: questions that require the systematic search for information in order to be answered

INFORMATION: facts that are easily coded into data

EXPERTS: those adept in finding answers to technical questions

TECHNICAL QUESTIONS

We can call questions that require the acquisition and analysis of information to be satisfactorily answered "technical questions." These questions are usually of such enormity that they have traditionally required whole armies of fact-gathering and questionnaire-administering "experts" to answer them.

EVERYDAY QUESTIONS

big and little questions

* This sociological fact about questions—that they are increasingly owned and controlled by powerful experts—has made many of us feel that our own mundane, day-to-day questions are comparatively rather insignificant. Questions that can be answered without this kind of intensive searching for information can be called EVERYDAY QUESTIONS. The types of question I mentioned above, questions about telling the time, disciplining pets, meeting family obligations, and the like, fall into this category. Everyday questions are the questions that tend to clutter our minds for most of our waking lives; hence it seems on the face of things that the vast majority of all questions are everyday questions.

QUESTIONS IN CONFLICT

* We have now made an **important distinction**, one that is crucial if we are to get a grip on the nature and purpose of philosophy. THIS IS THE DISTINCTION BETWEEN THE "TECHNICAL" AND "THE EVERYDAY." Other common ways of understanding this distinction are to see it in terms of **"science versus common sense"** or **"control versus freedom"** or **"the state versus civil society."** For anybody to understand philosophy they must first see that these two kinds of questions are, in some sense, in conflict with one another.

will I ever be rich and famous?

THE DIVISION IN MODERN CULTURE

* What I want to suggest here is that, to all intents and purposes, there are only two basic types of question: **technical questions and everyday questions**. *Any question that is not a technical question is an everyday question and vice versa. This way of analytically dividing questions mirrors the fact that the modern world is, sociologically speaking, divided into two mutually antagonistic cultures, the expert and the "lay."* Most everyday questions are "lay" questions and we like to answer these questions for ourselves. We usually get very upset when others, especially experts, try to answer them for us.

Different worlds

The questions and insights that emerge from our everyday lives are radically different from those that emerge from technical sciences. In fact, the world of science and the everyday world of common sense stand in antagonistic relation to each other, and science has historically attempted to correct the deficiencies of ordinary common sense. For example, because of science, we no longer believe the sun orbits the earth, despite appearances.

THE POWER OF EXPERTS

★ It is probably fair to say that the most significant faith of the modern world is the belief that all the major problems of life can be solved by technical experts armed with their arsenals of technical skills. This faith, like all faiths, has its priestly caste and, as with all priestly castes, there is a central creed.

"Will the polar ice caps melt due to global warming?"

Power games

Many contemporary sociologists claim that modern societies are now information societies where political power lies with those who have sufficient financial and intellectual resources at their disposal to make effective use of information. Modern societies are thus preoccupied with technical questions, and power in modern societies increasingly resides in the hands of experts.

BEYOND TECHNOCRATS

★ The high priests of modernity believe that the only important and significant questions of human life are technical questions. For this reason these people are usually referred to as "technocrats."

★ This type of person believes that **most everyday questions are so mundane and trivial that it is really not worth examining them in any detail**. He or she is only interested in those everyday questions that are COMPLEX AND INSTRUCTIVE ENOUGH TO BE CONVERTED INTO TECHNICAL QUESTIONS.

experts— are they always right?

THE SIGNIFICANCE OF EVERYDAY QUESTIONS

* Thankfully, most of us still feel that our everyday questions are significant. They are certainly significant to us. AND SOMETIMES, NOW AND AGAIN, EVERYDAY QUESTIONS TAKE ON A SCALE AND A SIGNIFICANCE THAT SEEM TO DWARF ALL OTHER QUESTIONS COMPLETELY.

what is time?

* Sometimes, after we have wondered what the time is, we might be struck by the question, **"What is time?"** Occasionally, after deciding that we really ought to visit our mother, we might ask ourselves, **"How should I live my life?"** THESE QUESTIONS SEEM ALMOST BASIC. Let's call them the *fundamental questions of everyday life*. Clearly, these are not technical questions. **No amount of fact-gathering can answer this type of question.**

* In fact, we seem to have asked ourselves here A RADICALLY DIFFERENT KIND OF QUESTION, one that falls outside the technocrat's technical remit and one that will require an unusual approach if it is ever to receive an adequate answer.

common sense will shed light

KEY WORDS

TECHNOCRACY: societies ruled by technicians and administrators

TECHNOCRATS: high-powered, highly skilled technicians and administrators who are increasingly responsible for making the important decisions facing modern societies

COMMON SENSE: ordinary "everyday" knowledge about ourselves and our surroundings

EVERYDAY QUESTIONS: questions that emerge from ordinary common life; they can usually be answered by relying on common sense

PHILOSOPHICAL QUESTIONS

★ Questions that fall outside the technocrats' realm can be called philosophical questions. These are not concerned with acquiring information, but with something else—something we might call "wisdom." Philosophers are "lovers of wisdom."

the Greeks first examined their navel

EVERYONE IS A PHILOSOPHER

Philosophical questions are a special variety of everyday question. They stand alone among questions as the ones that aim to transcend our mundane concerns so that we can see the world and ourselves as they are, untainted by the pain and prejudice of our common lives. More importantly, because philosophical questions are everyday questions, everybody is, as the modern Italian philosopher Antonio Gramsci claimed, at some point in their life, a philosopher.

IT'S ALL GREEK

★ For most philosophers, possessing wisdom is commonly seen as being equivalent to knowing and being guided by the "truth." But the truth of the philosophers is not the habitual and unexamined truth that happens to be the fashionable opinion of the moment, a "truth" that is spun from the minds of politicians, or newspapermen, or career academics who wouldn't recognize the truth if it moved in next door. For to be a philosopher is to set yourself against "the opinion-lovers" (or "philodoxoi," as the Greeks called them) and to view such faddish truths as merely the commonly agreed upon lies of the time.

I always look for the truth

WHAT MAKES US HUMAN?

★ HOW HAS PHILOSOPHY TRIED TO ANSWER SUCH QUESTIONS? From a historical perspective, we can see that **philosophy has tried to answer questions using its own distinctive methods and approaches**. Usually, philosophers have attempted to answer this type of question by a process sometimes known as **reflection**. WHAT DO PHILOSOPHERS MEAN BY THIS? *Well, the human ability to reflect about the nature of themselves and their surroundings stems from the fact that human beings possess "self consciousness." It is this ability that allows us to "detach ourselves" from our immediate concerns and look at our surroundings in a more sober and dispassionate way.*

reflection—more than a mirror image

★ Our self-consciousness is clearly like having an **"internal mirror"** that allows us to MONITOR OUR OWN ACTIONS, THOUGHTS, AND PERCEPTIONS. For the philosophers, **reflection is just this "looking back" at ourselves**, but not out of a need for self-control (or vanity!), but out of the need for answers about the nature of human life itself.

Philosopher's requirements

You don't need to be an expert to be a philosopher. Although there are some philosophers who consider themselves experts on their subject, to do philosophy requires no prior experience or special training. All that is required is an open and enquiring frame of mind. Philosophy is the "discipline" devoted to the study of these fundamental questions of everyday life; as a "discipline," it aims to give sensible and coherent answers to these questions. But, to repeat, these answers don't necessarily aim to inform those who study them, not in the ordinary sense of the word, anyway. They are meant to guide you on to a higher or better way of understanding yourself and the world so that you can become wiser than you are.

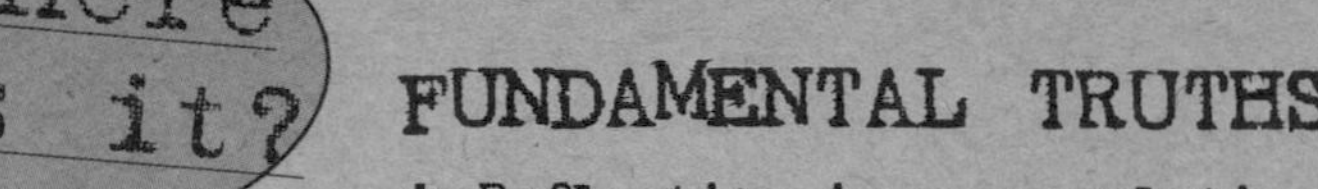

FUNDAMENTAL TRUTHS

where is that fundamental truth?

* Reflection is a speculative type of thinking that searches for the self-evident, the profoundly obvious, or, as philosophers are apt to put it, the necessary features of human life. That is, reflection is the type of thinking that searches for things in human life that must be true; it looks for the foundations or the fundamental presuppositions of all our everyday ways of being.

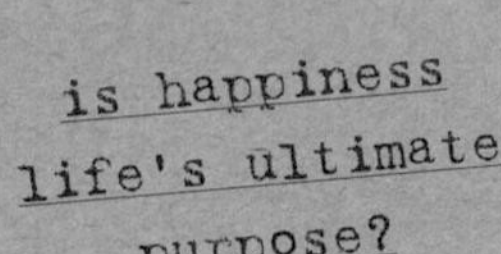

PROFOUND SIMPLICITIES

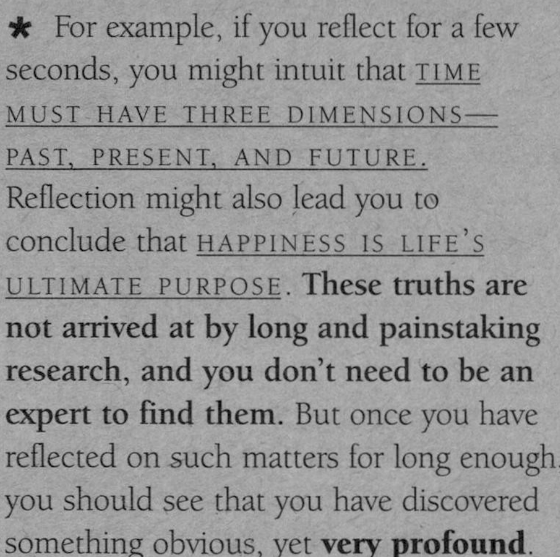

* For example, if you reflect for a few seconds, you might intuit that TIME MUST HAVE THREE DIMENSIONS—PAST, PRESENT, AND FUTURE. Reflection might also lead you to conclude that HAPPINESS IS LIFE'S ULTIMATE PURPOSE. **These truths are not arrived at by long and painstaking research, and you don't need to be an expert to find them.** But once you have reflected on such matters for long enough, you should see that you have discovered something obvious, yet **very profound**.

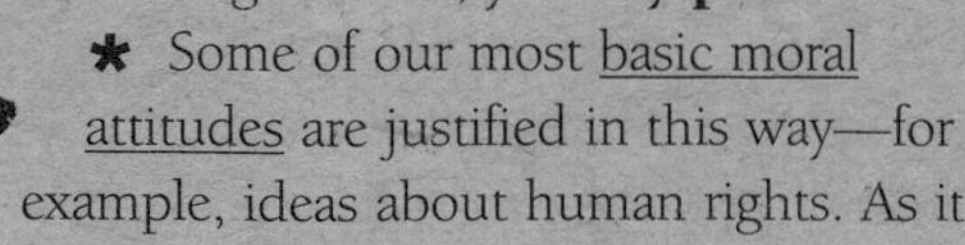

* Some of our most basic moral attitudes are justified in this way—for example, ideas about human rights. As it

states in The Declaration of Independence, **"we hold these truths to be self-evident,"** and it is REFLECTIVE THINKING that allows us to make such strong assertions.

well that's the business of philosophy out of the way

BEYOND INFORMATION

* **Philosophical questions are some of the most fundamental questions of everyday life.** They are not technical questions and cannot be answered in the same way as technical questions—that is, by so-called experts. They are questions that arise out of the problems of everyday existence, and they can seem so strange and baffling as to almost defy explanation.

* But some people have attempted to answer them. By reflecting deeply on this kind of question, some people have endeavored to go beyond the quest for **"mere information"** and have set off in pursuit of a higher, "wiser," state of being.

THE STORY OF PHILOSOPHY

This book is the story of how philosophers have struggled to attain wisdom. Some have lost their minds in this effort, some have been persecuted, and others have become powerful and politically influential figures. This story of philosophy is a story of the wonder of human questioning. If you feel dissatisfied and disenchanted with the way the modern world provides answers to its big questions, then you are well on your way to becoming a philosopher.

philosophy: a new way of looking

how many philosophers does it take to change a light bulb?

ASK A SILLY QUESTION

★ Questions need not be classified solely in terms of their size or how informative they are, as the technocrat tries to. Questions can be classified according to how silly they are. We have all asked and been asked some very stupid questions, and we have usually experienced some embarrassment as a consequence. Some people—let's call them philistines—believe that philosophical questions are of this type.

A WASTE OF TIME

★ *For the philistine, philosophical questions are just plain stupid*. They are the kind of questions a child would ask, and anyone who wanders around with questions like that on their mind is bound to run into trouble fairly quickly. Put simply, answers to philosophical questions don't pay the bills, mend the broken fence, or improve your sex life, so why bother with them?

★ Only a fool or a child would waste their valuable time on such pointlessness, and, in the eyes of the philistine, the philosopher is both.

philosophers are worse than silly children

ATTACK OF THE PHILISTINES

*** For the philistine, it is everyday, practical questions that are important,** not intellectual ones. The technocrat and the philosopher are accused of over-intellectualizing and creating problems where none, in reality, exist.

* THE PHILISTINE WORSHIPS AT THE ALTAR OF COMMON SENSE, and both the technocrat and the philosopher tend to be viewed as **intellectual infidels.** These people have to be perpetually crusaded against to prevent their **garbage from polluting the wells of ordinary, workaday existence.**

ARE PHILOSOPHERS SLACKERS?

* The reason for the philistine's particular grudge against philosophy is that philosophical questions are seen as the kind of questions raised by immature, lazy, intellectual slackers who lie around all day thinking and generally indulging themselves. For the hard-working philistines of this world, nothing is worse than idleness and futility. Get rid of these loafers and the world will be a much better place, says the philistine. What are we to make of these claims?

get a proper job, you idle philosopher

Philistines

The word "philistine" originated in eighteenth-century Germany where students referred to uneducated townspeople as "philisters." Since then the word has customarily been used to refer to those people who are insensitive to all things cultural.

life's a struggle, there's no time for philosophy

KEY WORDS

SILLY QUESTIONS: pointless and worthless questions that do not make sense

PHILISTINES: champions of common sense who think that many technocrats and most philosophers ask silly questions

EVERYDAY WONDER

***** The famous Austrian philosopher Ludwig Wittgenstein (more on him later) once wrote "philosophy begins with wonder," and it is in those strange moments of everyday wonder that philosophical questions have their origin. This sense of wonder about ourselves and the world does contain the residues of a childlike innocence.

PICTURE THIS

To wonder is to be driven by a particular type of curiosity. When we wonder about ourselves and our surroundings we allow ourselves to be guided by imaginative ideas. These help us speculate about the best way of understanding ourselves and our surroundings. Coleridge, one of the Romantic poets of the nineteenth century, believed that this way of thinking was the "living power and prime agent of all human perception."

CHILDLIKE CURIOSITY

***** Some philosophers, the contemporary American philosopher WILLARD VAN ORMAN QUINE for example (as we shall see, philosophers often have quite striking names), have, like the philistine, **drawn the comparison between the type of questions philosophers ask and the type of questions children ask**. And we would have to admit there is a NOTICEABLE SIMILARITY HERE.

***** All of us have been lost for words when asked a **"what is"** question by a small child. Questions like, **"Mommy, what are colors?"** or, **"Daddy, what are dreams?"** are usually met with evasive and half-hearted answers by bewildered parents. The philosopher would have to say that there is some merit to the philistine's case.

WHERE'S THE WONDER?

★ However, the philistine's view suffers from a more serious limitation: **while the philosopher can understand the philistine's point of view, the philistine simply cannot understand the philosopher's**. This is because the philistine's mind is essentially CLOSED and the philistine approaches the world with a NARROW-MINDEDNESS that in effect takes the world as it is entirely for granted.

HOPEFUL THINKING

★ The philosopher says that there are reasons for why the world is as it is. And questioning why the world is like this might give us some ideas as to how to make it better.

The kingdom of philosophy

To do philosophy, then, requires a certain amount childlike wonder at the world—a kind of permanent astonishment at those things that most people simply take for granted. To enter the kingdom of philosophy, one must become like a child again and it is easier for a double-decker bus to pass through a key hole than it is for a technocrat or philistine to enter the kingdom of philosophy. And so much the worse for them, says the philosopher.

PHILOSOPHICAL TYPES

To complicate matters further, philosophers ask different types of questions, and the type of philosophical question asked defines the philosopher. Very briefly, there are four types of philosophical questions and so there are four basic types of philosopher.

WHAT AND HOW?

* First, there are questions about the basic nature of things, what things really are. These are called **metaphysical questions**. For example the question, "What is time?" is a good example of a metaphysical question because it is asking what time really is.

* Second, there are questions that turn on notions of knowledge or belief. These questions are known as **epistemological questions** and they focus not on what there is (which is a metaphysical concern) but how we can know about what there is.

* For example, **if someone claimed that the world had been invaded by aliens you might justifiably**

KEY WORDS

METAPHYSICS: philosophy that attempts to catalog and define everything that exists

EPISTEMOLOGY: philosophy that attempts to account for how individuals can know about what exists

ETHICS: philosophy that defines the nature of the "good life"

POLITICS: the study of the ideal form of human society

ask them, "HOW DO YOU KNOW?" *If they then went on to say that they knew this because they dreamt last night that a large flying saucer had landed in their backyard, then you would probably feel justified in dismissing them as a nutcase.*

* This is because most people now believe that dreams are not a reliable source of knowledge, and epistemology examines what kinds of experiences are reliable sources of knowledge.

should we always believe what we are told or must we question it?

ETHICS AND POLITICS

* Third, there are questions about the nature of the good or virtuous life. These questions are called **ethical questions** and they focus on the moral problem of how we ought to live our lives. *Most of us have given these questions some consideration and so most of us are already reasonably competent moral philosophers.*

* Finally, there are questions of the nature of the just society; that is, ideally, how any human society should be organized. Those who raise these questions are called **political philosophers**.

mr. and mrs. alien invite you to their barbecue on Saturday

HISTORY LESSON

Philosophy is usually divided into four historical periods: classical, medieval, modern, and post-modern. Modern philosophy is usually claimed to have its roots in the sixteenth century philoso-phizings of René Descartes and Thomas Hobbes. Postmodern philosophy has its roots in the radical ideas that emerged out of 1960s counter-cultures.

PHILOSOPHY'S STRUGGLE

★ We now have the characters of our story: the technocrats, the philistines, and the philosophers. Now we need a plot. The plot is a simple one. It is the effort of the technocrats and philistines to undermine philosophy. Why? Because the technocrats and philistines both believe in the values of order, and philosophy's questioning attitude is sometimes mistakenly seen as attacking civilization as we know it.

Plato

SCHOOL'S IN

Philosophy, as we Westerners understand it, is about 2,700 years old. It was the Greeks who, some three millennia ago, began to record the human interest in philosophical questions, and they formed loose associations of individuals who thought about philosophical issues in a similar way. This is what we mean by a school of philosophy.

WHERE IT ALL BEGAN

★ There are seven parts to this story. Chapter one, entitled *"Magic and Metaphysics,"* is the story of how philosophy emerged out of what was essentially a religious sensibility and went on to play a central role in the development of some of our most basic ways of understanding the world.

★ Chapter two, *"Truth and Opinion,"* is the story of how **Plato**, who, as you will see, is something of a villain in this book, developed an account of the nature of the true and just social order. For Plato, the ideal society is one that systematically excludes large sections of humanity and exposes the rest to harsh forms of social control.

a seven-act play

★ PLATO WAS THUS THE FIRST THINKER OF NOTE TO PRODUCE A BLUEPRINT FOR A TECHNOCRATIC SOCIETY.

CLASH OF THE TITANS

* Chapter three, *"God and the Universe,"* is the story of how **Aristotle's** ideas were used by the Catholic Church to construct the medieval view of the world and how the values of the classical world were transformed by their encounter with RADICAL JUDAISM AND ROMAN PAGANISM. In particular, this chapter discusses how questions of ethics increasingly began to replace questions of "truth" and "justice" as the central concerns of philosophers after the fall of the Roman Empire.

IT'S THOSE PHILISTINES AGAIN

* Chapter four, *"The Rise of the Technocrats,"* charts the origins and the subsequent development of the "philosophies" of science and mathematics from the **Enlightenment** to the present day. It is a story of how modern technocrats have developed technically oriented "philosophies" that have allowed them to intensify their efforts to predict and control the world.

* Chapter five, *"Romantics and Revolutionaries,"* sketches the rise of the cultural movements, originating in the early part of the nineteenth century, that attempted to EXPOSE THE EXPONENTS OF PHILISTINISM AND TECHNOCRACY TO A PHILOSOPHICAL CRITIQUE. This chapter outlines the ways in which these critiques have been appropriated by the philistines and the technocrats for their own ends.

Aristotle

Who are the philosophers?

Philosophy touches on all areas of human life in that it asks metaphysical, epistemological, ethical, and political questions. But this all-pervasiveness of philosophical questions can make philosophers indistinguishable from the crowd. This problem of "identity" (who and where are the philosophers?) is becoming one of the key questions contemporary philosophers have to address.

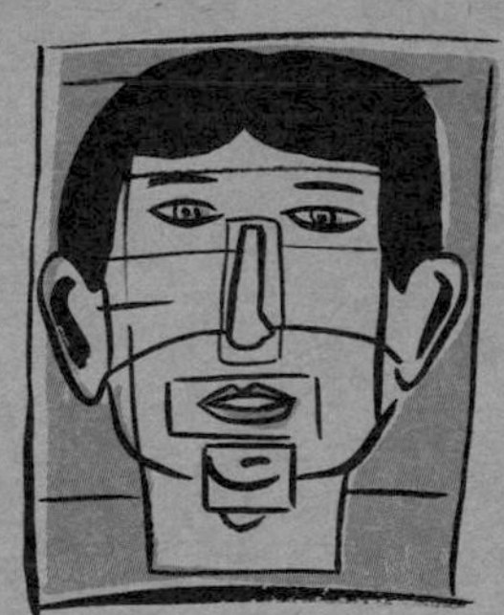

have you seen this man?

WHAT THE FUTURE HOLDS

what does the future hold?

★ The last part of the book is about now. Chapter six, "Endgames," discusses the state of philosophy in the twentieth century, focusing on those philosophers who claim that philosophy is now near its end. The final chapter, "It's a Wonderful Life?," considers the prospects for the future of philosophy and tries to show how philosophizing is not only intrinsically interesting, but is a vital part of any culture that can justifiably claim to allow people to live a meaningful life.

REASSURANCE FOR PHILOSOPHOBICS

★ Since the history of philosophy extends over thousands of years, you would need several very big books to do justice to its diversity. To simplify matters, I have written a relatively simple historical account of the emergence of Western philosophy and its subsequent long and painful decline.

it's my book and I'll write what I want

★ I have also attempted to make what are sometimes difficult and esoteric philosophical ideas as friendly as possible. In fact, this book should, I hope, read like an informal conversation so that you can engage with the book in the relaxed and open manner in which you conduct your day-to-day conversations (with people you like, anyway!).

* However, the very idea of reading a book about philosophy can fill even the most open-minded of people with feelings of dread and foreboding. To help those who are philosophically phobic in this way, I recommend that you practice some self-relaxation techniques before you start reading. Here's one for you to try …

let me tell you the story of philosophy...

JUST RELAX...

* Lie down, close your eyes and concentrate on the sound of your own breathing. Imagine you are to be told a story by an old man who claims to be a philosopher. Picture this man in your mind. Once you have done this, jump up and start reading this book straight away.

Come back Philosophy

Philosophy has, historically, been passive in the face of attacks against it and, as a result, is now on the verge of extinction as a discipline in the modern academy. Now is the time to fight back and to expose those people who espouse "philosophies" that make you hate yourself and hate life. Any philosophy that is worthy of the name should be about liberating us from these dark phantoms of the modern age.

Apologia

Since this is a very short book, I have had to ignore the lives and the work of some interesting philosophers. I apologize if your favorite philosopher is missing, but I had to make some difficult choices about the content of this book. Such is the way in philosophy.

CHAPTER 1

MAGIC AND METAPHYSICS

* How appropriate that the story of philosophy should begin with some big questions. Several such questions clearly spring to mind at the start of our journey. Where and when did philosophical forms of questioning originate? How and why did this type of questioning appear and what effects did the emergence of philosophy have on the culture and society of the time?

STANLEY CAVELL

The modern American philosopher Stanley Cavell has claimed that philosophical questions are a response to a real experience that can take hold of human beings at anytime. However, it was the ancient Greeks who were the first to clearly articulate these experiences and to systematically try to find answers to the questions they seemed to raise.

IT STARTED IN THE MEDITERRANEAN

* To answer these questions, WE MUST GO BACK TO A TIME BEFORE PHILOSOPHY (B.P.) and see how prephilosophical cultures differed from those cultures, like ours, that have been thoroughly imbued with the philosophical spirit.

* *Some 2,700 years ago in the Greek-speaking colonies on the coast of what is now Turkey, there emerged a particular and peculiar way of thinking about humans and their environment that was to have an enormous significance for the future course of world history.* This new way of thinking emerged from the new and radically different kinds of questions that some

people were prepared to ask. To put the matter simply, certain individuals began to wonder what things in themselves really were. This new sense of wonder about the world was the catalytic source from which all subsequent metaphysical types of question were derived. Hence metaphysics, as we in the West understand the term, begins with the thoughts of these ancient Greeks.

IN THE BEGINNING

* The questions asked by early GREEK PHILOSOPHERS still appear philosophically relevant today. Even those of us who value our own decidedly modern sensibilities can still find nourishment in these early philosophizings.
* Although philosophical ways of thinking emerged at around the same time in Persia, India, and China, it is the Greeks who most clearly bequeathed to the modern world its most valued philosophical inheritance.

I am the walrus

ANCIENT MAGIC

Ancient magic worked according to two principles: **mimesis**, or the idea that a person could take on the power of a particular person or thing by imitating it, and **contagion**, that the power of a particular person or thing could be transmitted by simple contact with it.

a time before philosophy

a shaman

MAGICAL CULTURES

★ Prior to the arrival of Greek ways of thinking in Europe, it is fair to say that the bulk of everyday thinking was magical. I don't mean that prephilosophical peoples went around sawing other people in half or pulling rabbits out of hats or anything like that. No, what I am trying to say is that prephilosophical people relied more on wishes, dreams, and omens than on questions as the means of organizing and directing their lives.

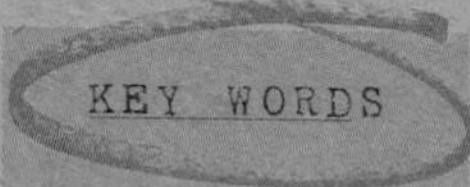

MAGIC: ancient technique for controlling the world by making representations of it

SHAMAN: person adept in the art of ancient magic

MODERNIST: person who claims that magic is hokum and that reason, science, and logic should guide our lives

MAGIC VS. REASON

★ In magical cultures, people tended to think that they could control events simply by wishing that events would turn out a particular way. Hence, magic-based cultures tended to rely on ways of thinking that dealt in the currency of wishes.

★ This differs from the typical thoughts of the typical **modernist** in some stark and significant ways. For example, if we want to move house, we might make some calculations about cost, look at how the area in which the house is situated is served by local amenities, and so on. In modern cultures, as we shall discuss later, people tend to

howz zat!

make these kind of rational calculations when forced into making important decisions.

★ However, these rational thought processes are a relatively recent invention, and for thousands of years B.P. rationality was an exceptional and vastly under-utilized mode of thought. (In fact, as you will see later, the ability to think rationally has become something of an entry requirement for those willing to participate in the modern world, and certain technocratic "philosophers" have helped to legitimize these rational ways of thinking as the only true ways of thinking.)

WORLDS OF ENCHANTMENT

★ We can draw some important conclusions about the nature of pre-philosophical societies from the character of these forms of decision-making. Firstly, because magical messages could be read from almost any object deemed sacred enough to display them, the world B.P. was clearly an enchanted world in comparison with our own. It was a world that was animated with spirits, both good and bad, and these spirits communicated with humans in a language that was only legible to the initiated few.

★ This special group of people who could read and speak the magical languages of the spirit world were known as **shamans**.

the gods ran the show

THE WORLD BEFORE PHILOSOPHY

The prephilosophical world was a world where people viewed themselves as being inseparable from their natural surroundings. Pre-philosophical peoples believed they could use nature's power by making "imitative representations" of nature in the form of sketches and effigies.

SHAMANIC WISDOM

★ Shamans were the point of magical connection between the spirit and human worlds, and so they were like an early type of priesthood and therefore a site of significant political power. Since magical information was needed to solve important, everyday problems, most people's lives were essentially controlled by those who professed some fluency in the occult languages of magic.

Adolf Hitler: a ruthless despot

Residual magic

Just think how many times a day you behave superstitiously: touching wood, crossing your fingers, or saluting magpies. Each time you do something like this, you let a little residual magic into your world, a form of thinking that represents an echo in the present from an ancient, pagan, pre-philosophical past.

magpies—one for sorrow, two for joy

POWER AND SACRIFICE

★ Magical cultures were, in all probability, a little like Nazi Germany in the 1930s (more on this later, too) in that they were probably ruled by ruthless despots who governed by convincing the mass of the population that they could only be saved from destruction by submitting to their magical authority.

★ Two important features of pre-philosophical cultures follow from all this. First, these cultures were extremely hierarchical in comparison to our own; those in power had lots of power and those without it had almost none and could see no easy way of attaining any. Second, and relatedly, because the great spirit or spirits were seen as being all-pervasive, that is, capable of penetrating and influencing all things, even individual humans were ultimately subject to magical control. This means that prephilosophical cultures had no concept of "an individual" in the sense that we have when we use the term "individual person." In these cultures, the individual was subordinate to the whole; everything was, in some sense, interconnected with everything else in a great enchanted chain of being. For this reason, it was deemed perfectly acceptable to sacrifice small children for the sake of the well-being of everyone else.

MAGICAL THINKING TODAY

* These cultures, interestingly, have never completely disappeared, and forms of magical thinking continue to haunt the minds of even the most ultra-rational modernist. Today there are still contemporary cultures that interpret the world in essentially magical ways.
* Some of the neopagan youth subcultures that have become increasingly popular in recent years still value this way of thinking and continue to practice magic for healing and to enhance general psychological well-being. The fact that magical ways of thinking have never been completely eliminated suggests that they service a need that their more cold and rational modern counterparts simply cannot meet.

PAGANISM

The original pagan cultures, with their matriarchal spirituality, were radically undermined with the invasion of southern Europe by Greek-speaking warriors from the East some 3,200 years ago. They brought with them their deeply patriarchal culture and religion and placed their great sky-god Zeus at the head of the sacred pagan spiritual hierarchy.

druids at work

The new religion

From magic came religion. The magical forces of the spirit world gave way to the more detached powers of the gods. Paganism continued, but its spirits played second fiddle to the new pantheon of Greek deities.

Thales

One of the first philosophers was Thales "the Wise" (c.620–c.555 B.C.). He understood his external surroundings as an ordered cosmos.

Thales the Wise

KEY WORDS

WONDER: an attitude of openness to the world that allowed a new intellectual intimacy with things
SPECULATION: the art of imaginative guessing about the true nature of things
PHUSIS: the underlying principles of the cosmos that govern how things emerge and decay

GREEK GODS TAKE OVER

★ The Greek gods were more detached and impersonal than the Pagan Earth spirits. They remained transcendentally aloof from human concerns, so the kinds of shamanic communion typical of pagan cultures was not possible with the Greek gods. They controlled human events from their Olympian heights, meaning that, increasingly, much of the human drama below was seen by most people as being outside of human control. People saw their lives as fated by the whims of the gods.

A SIGNIFICANT SHIFT

★ The emergence of philosophy changed all this. The personalized universe of gods and spirits was replaced by something very different, and the world has never been quite the same since. While pagan cultures viewed the external world as essentially one "great you" or "big Other" to be coaxed and cajoled into revealing its sacred mysteries, philosophy viewed the world as an impersonal "it" to be speculated on, reimagined, and openly interpreted. This helped change the whole character of ancient human experience. The prephilosophical world of spirits and gods could be an extremely frightening place for the powerless mass of the population. Philosophy introduced ways of thinking that offered people an escape from these misplaced fears. The world became an object of detached human contemplation which, as we know, can be a very soothing and calming way of looking at things. The world became something for us to appreciate and interpret, and this represented something of an evolutionary moment in the history of the human mind.

"ground control to Major Tom"

COSMOPOLITAN MILETUS

* All this started in Miletus, a port on the shores of Asia Minor in a region called Ionia. Why philosophy should have started here is anybody's guess. Perhaps it had something to do with the cosmopolitan nature of this part of the Greek-speaking empire, where Greek and Persian cultures met. Some individuals might have become disenchanted with traditional forms of religious authority that used ideas of the sacred and the divine for self-serving and unenlightened purposes.

Apollo

Past imperfect

The early Ionian philosophers saw the human mind as having the power to step back and create an image of the external world as it is. These philosophers claimed that this cosmos operated according to its own principles (phusis) that existed independently of human custom and tradition (nomos). The separation of the cosmos from the human psyche is what enabled these pre-Socratic (before Socrates) philosophers to reflect speculatively on the true nature of the cosmos and to offer new ways of seeing the world that broke with magical traditions of the past.

KEY WORDS

PRE-SOCRATICS: Greek philosophers before Socrates who attempted to poetically describe the true nature of the cosmos

COSMOS: the idea that the universe is an ordered whole

LOGOS: the fundamental principle that governs the "working" of the cosmos

WHAT IS IT?

* It seems that the first philosophical question ever to be asked was the metaphysical question, "What is it?" "It," the cosmos, was understood as separate from, yet part of, humanity. It becomes for the first time an object of wonder and benign curiosity. For Thales, the cosmos was fundamentally like a substance—water. This really isn't as silly a speculation as it sounds. Water is essential for complex forms of life to exist, so for someone living by the sea, this is a pretty intelligent first guess as to the nature of the great "it" of the cosmos.

I see no ships

what is the cosmos?

THE INFINITE COSMIC FORCE

* For THALES' PUPIL ANAXIMANDER (611–547 B.C.), everything in the cosmos originates from "**the infinite**"; a kind of unlimited and everlasting cosmic force. For his pupil ANAXIMINES (died c. 500 B.C.), everything consisted of **air**.

* The cosmos for these philosophers retained a spiritual feel, and so pre-Socratic philosophy is much more than a simple rationalization of pagan magic. On the contrary, it retains something of this magic while refusing to submit to its authority.

CREATIVE CONTRADICTIONS

* We can see the tension between the rational and the magical in pre-Socratic thought most clearly in the writings of the greatest of the Ionian philosophers, HERACLITUS OF EPHESUS (died 460 B.C.). His concern, like that of his Ionian predecessors, was with the fundamental nature of the cosmos, but for Heraclitus, these speculations become more profound. What interested him was the meaning of the cosmos, or its **logos**.

wow, look at that view!

* The logos, for HERACLITUS, is a single unified principle that implies that, in some sense, the cosmos is one single and unified thing. But at the same time this principle turns back on itself and contradicts itself, like the figures in an Escher drawing.

Dynamic flux

Heraclitus' metaphysics states that the entire cosmos operates according to a simple **dynamic principle** that maintained the universe in a state of harmony. However, Heraclitan harmony was more akin to a state of perpetual war than blissful tranquility. For him, the cosmos was a continually moving unity-in-opposition driven by cosmic antagonism and contradiction.

and another thing...

COSMOLOGY

As the early Ionian philosophers were speculating about the nature of the cosmos, they can be viewed as the founders of modern day cosmology.

HERACLITUS' COSMOS

★ In Heraclitus' metaphysics, the cosmos is dynamic, driven by contradictions at the heart of the cosmic logos. This means that change and flux are at the core of his metaphysics and, as a result, his ideas have been influential in the philosophy of history. Both of the modern philosophers Hegel and Heidegger acknowledge a debt to his thought (more on them later).

PADDLING IN RIVERS

Heraclitus is famous for claiming that "you never step in the same river twice." What he meant by this was that change is intrinsic to the cosmos and that each event in time is unique.

EVER-LIVING FIRE

★ To cope with his idea of a dynamic logos, Heraclitus had to find a picture of the fundamental nature of his cosmos that was compatible with the dynamic logos. He speculated that the cosmos was **"an ever-living fire, kindling in measures and being extinguished in measures."** So although Heraclitus tried to understand the rational logos of the cosmos, he also believed that the entire cosmos was in some sense **alive**. His world was both RATIONAL AND MAGICAL AT THE SAME TIME. This feature of his philosophy is hard for us moderns to understand.

Parmenides

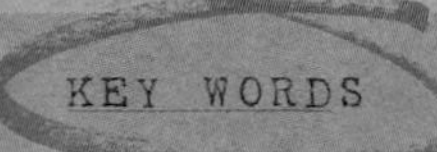

KEY WORDS

MONISM:
the metaphysical idea that the cosmos is made of one kind of stuff

PLURALISM:
the idea that the cosmos is made of different kinds of stuff

ARGUMENT EMERGES

* At around the same time (500 B.C.) at the far western edge of the Greek-speaking world, A RIVAL PHILOSOPHICAL SCHOOL WAS BEING FOUNDED BY PARMENIDES (see pages 40–43) in the southern Italian town of **Elea**.

we're all unique, darling

an ever-living fire, kindling in measures and being extinguished in measures

PARMENIDES

Parmenides is often (falsely) credited as the originator of a distinctive metaphysical position, monism, or the belief that everything is, in reality, one single kind of thing. Thus his ideas and those of his imitators such as Melissus are often termed "Eleatic (from Elea) monism"

but I've got logical proof

but the cosmos has never moved or changed

* For Parmenides, the cosmos, despite appearances, never moved or changed. He was the first to try to prove this rather **counter-intuitive conclusion** by means of a logical proof. IT IS WITH PARMENIDES THAT PHILOSOPHY BEGINS TO RELY ON ARGUMENT TO JUSTIFY ITS SPECULATIONS.

PARMENIDES OF ELEA

* Parmenides was a contemporary of Heraclitus, but they lived at opposite ends of the Greek world. There is no evidence that they ever met, although some scholars mistakenly suggest that Parmenides' philosophy is an explicit refutation of its Ionian counterpart. We know from Plato's writings that Parmenides visited Athens late in his life, where he met the young Socrates (469-399 B.C.) for whom he was to prove a significant influence.

PARMENIDES

Parmenides (c.515–c.445 B.C.) was the first European philosopher to be concerned with the most fundamental of fundamental questions—"What does it mean to be?" He was probably a Pythagorean and his philosophy retains something of this school's Orphic mysticism.

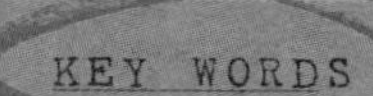

KEY WORDS

BEING:
what all truly existing things possess

NOTHING:
the absence of being

ORPHIC:
pertaining to ancient Greek mystery religions

THE ARTISTIC TYPE

* Like all the other pre-Socratic philosophers, **Parmenides'** philosophy was expressed in the form of a poem. This shows that, for these early philosophers, philosophical questions arose out of an artistic rather than a scientific temperament and that we need to read their philosophical texts **metaphorically** rather than **literally**.

For this reason, Parmenides' philosophy, like those of the other pre-Socratics, cannot be compared easily with modern philosophies that have their roots in a more literally-minded technological culture.

PARMENIDES' DREAM

★ Parmenides' philosophy is an account of a dream. In his dream, Parmenides is trapped in the "dreadful house of black-robed night" when he is visited by a goddess who instructs him to find the way to the light of **the truth**. The Goddess states that there are two ways to all life: THE WAY OF IT IS AND THE WAY OF IT IS NOT.

Parmenides' dream

★ The way of "it is" is the way of truth that leads out of the darkness. The way of "it is not" is no real way at all, according to the goddess. It is the way of nothing rather than something, and "nothing" cannot be known. This way cannot be illuminated by the light of being, and it remains the way of darkness and nonbeing.

Kierkegaard

Kierkegaard

For Parmenides, the way of human life is an either–or; a fundamental choice between being and non-being. To this extent, he is similar to the modern philosopher Sören Kierkegaard (1813–55) and his existentialist imitators. According to this type of philosophy, you have to choose one way or the other in life. The moment of choice is the moment when your life really begins; prior to this you were not really existing at all.

ULTIMATE CHOICE

* Parmenides is not left alone to make the ultimate choice for himself, and the goddess urges him to choose the way of "it is." According to the fantastic wisdom of his divine apparition, if you choose the way of "it is not" then you are debarred from thought. For thought cannot be about "what is not" but only about "what is," which is to say that "thought and being are the same."

it's my life and I'll decide

be careful to choose the right way to think

remember the true nature of being

the goddess warns the philistines

THE WAY OF MORTALS

* The goddess also warns against another false way, the way of opinion, which she thinks is the way of most mortals. According to this way, the way of **"it is"** and the way of **"it is not"** are viewed as being the same, and ordinary mortals thus provide a name for the way of "it is not."

* It is here, according to the goddess that mortals have gone astray and have forgotten the true nature of being. Those who walk the **"way of opinion"** have forgotten that there are two distinct modes of existence and live in state of forgetfulness about being.

★ The conclusion Parmenides draws about the nature of being from this DIVINE EXERCISE IN METAPHYSICS is that being must be **"pure"** and **"unchanging."** *If being changed, it would have to become what "it is not," which is impossible because being is. Therefore, all change is an illusion, and the true reality of the cosmos is timeless and unchanging.*

DISPUTE RAGES

There is still some dispute among contemporary philosophers as to the real meaning of pre-Socratic thought. Some philosophers argue that the pre-Socratics were amateur scientists who were trying primitively to explain the cosmos. Others see them as more like magicians who were concerned with teaching, healing, and predicting the future.

PARMENIDES' LEGACY

★ The influence of Parmenides' philosophy is so important that it is hard to do it justice. Philosophers praise him for opening up the whole question of the TRUE NATURE OF HUMAN EXISTENCE. He can therefore be viewed as an early moral philosopher who asked profound and sincere ethical questions such as **"How should we live?"** In his opinion, this question can only be answered by first answering the question of the SIGNIFICANCE of human being.

★ Technocratic "philosophers," although they find Parmenides' philosophical style obscure and irritating, generally respect his attempts to look behind the false world of everyday opinion and ascertain the true structure of things in themselves. He is generally viewed by these "philosophers" as the founder of **metaphysical monism**, or the idea that everything is in reality made of one single stuff.

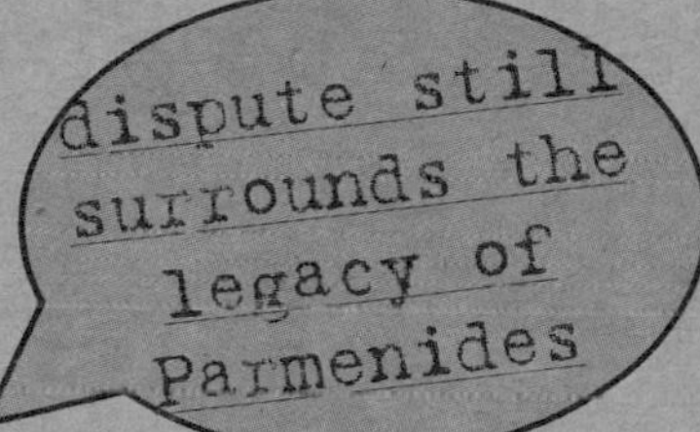

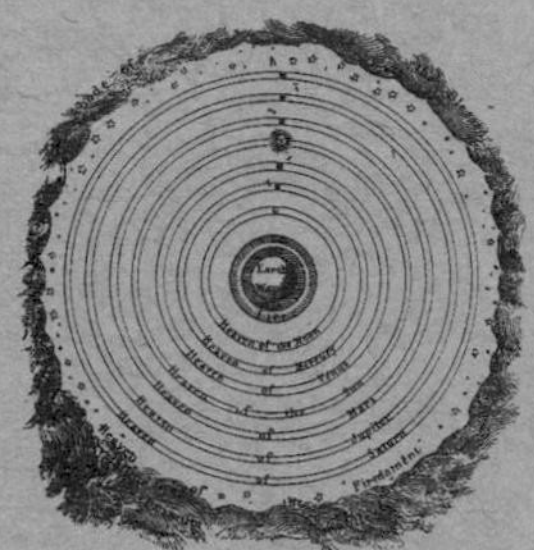

nominalists believe that appearance and reality are the same

MODERN PHYSICS

Modern physics, in its attempt to search for a single unified theory that explains the whole universe, strives after a metaphysical monism. On the other hand, our everyday ways of thinking about the cosmos tend to emphasize its diversity and so reflect a more pluralistic metaphysics.

can't you get it into your head?

THE NATURE OF THE COSMOS

* The pre-Socratics' speculations laid the foundations for a variety of basic conceptualizations that are still in use today. The first of these is the metaphysical distinction between "the one" and "the many." Is the cosmos really one thing or is it many different and diverse things? Those who see the cosmos as the former are called monists and those who opt for the latter are called metaphysical pluralists.

APPEARANCE AND REALITY

* In addition to this **metaphysical** scheme, the pre-Socratics also helped INSTITUTE ANOTHER BASIC METAPHYSICAL DISTINCTION *that is now part of our common-sense way of looking at the world.*
* This is the distinction between **appearance** and **reality**. For the pre-Socratics, the TRUE NATURE OF THE COSMOS was not as it appeared to unaided human senses. *The reality of the cosmos was somehow hidden behind the way it appeared, and was only made humanly accessible by means of a deeper, more reflective way of interpreting it.*

* The distinction between appearance and reality has become one of the most important and controversial distinctions in the history of metaphysics and, as we shall see, remains a source of many philosophical confusions.

SCIENCE NOW

* Those **metaphysicians** who believe that the true reality of the cosmos lies behind its appearances are known as **realists**. Most modern physicists subscribe to a metaphysical view of the world known as **scientific realism**, or the idea that our best scientific theories give us the true picture of the world. *Those who deny that such a reality exists beyond the way ordinary phenomena appear to us are sometimes called* **nominalists**, *because they believe that abstract ideas, such as those espoused by metaphysicians, exist in name only.*

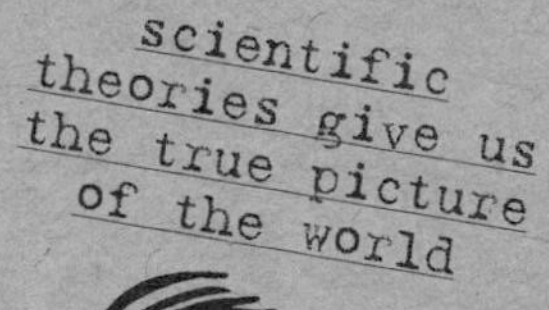

KEY WORDS

REALISTS: philosophers who believe that the real world (as it is in itself) is not as it appears to the senses
NOMINALISTS: philosophers who deny that there is reality to the world (as it is in itself) and claim that the world is as it is described by us

INFLUENTIAL IDEAS

* We can now see just how significant the thoughts of the pre-Socratics were. However, those philosophers writing after the Ionians and the Eleatics helped to develop metaphysical accounts of the cosmos that have proved to be even more influential.

DEMOCRITUS

Democritus (c.460–c.370 B.C.) speculated that the cosmos might consist of atoms and the void, and this has provided the philosophical foundation for modern physics and chemistry.

VOLCANIC PHILOSOPHY

* **Empedocles**, (c.490– c.430 B.C.) speculated that the COSMOS WAS COMPOSED OF FOUR BASIC ELEMENTS: EARTH, AIR, FIRE, AND WATER, and that the whole of reality consisted of a mixture of these elements. Because everything was a mixture of everything else, he believed that nothing could really be destroyed; it could only be recombined into a new type of thing.

* To test his theory, Empedocles jumped into the crater of Etna, a Sicilian mountain that remains an active volcano to this day, and became one with the lava. I guess you could say that he was a bit mixed up.

Empedocles' fiery finale

MATH IS THE KEY

* Another famous pre-Socratic whose ideas were to prove influential was **Pythagoras**. PYTHAGORAS AND HIS FOLLOWERS BELIEVED THAT THE COSMOS WAS ESSENTIALLY MUSICAL AND THAT THE UNIVERSE COULD BE UNDERSTOOD AS A PIECE OF MUSIC: that is, it can be represented in terms of simple mathematical ratios or harmonies. Pythagoras, as is now well known, pioneered the study of **geometry** and he looked for the simple and eternal mathematical relationships that exist in nature.

* PYTHAGORAS STARTED A RELIGIOUS CULT BASED ON HIS METAPHYSICAL IDEAS: he believed in the immortal soul, reincarnation, and that the good life can only be attained by living according to harmonious mathematical principles. His idea that truth lay in the appreciation of the pure and crystalline world of mathematics would later **influence Plato**.

PHILOSOPHY BECOMES POPULAR

* We are now about to enter a DECISIVE EPISODE IN THE HISTORY OF PHILOSOPHY. In this period, the so-called "Greek Enlightenment," the spirit of philosophical curiosity helps create a new intellectual climate. Out of this new interest in philosophical questions some recognizably modern forms of thinking would emerge.

Pythagoras

Pythagoras was the first philosopher to be concerned with the nature of the human soul. He believed in reincarnation, practiced strict vegetarianism, and gave lectures in a cave from behind a curtain.

Tee hee

ha ha ha

Democritus, the laughing philosopher

A HAPPY MAN

Democritus was the founder of a new and powerful metaphysics, **atomism**. This amused him so much it earned him the title the "laughing philosopher," although most people have failed to get the joke.

THE ATHENIAN INFLUENCE

★ During the fifth century, Athens extended its imperial influence throughout the Mediterranean. This enabled Athenians to enslave large numbers of their colonists and to subject them to forced labor. This gave the growing Athenian middle class more time and resources than they could cope with, so they filled their time with politics and philosophical speculation.

you dig and
I'll think

TRUTH?

For the Athenians, to be governed by **nous (the cosmic mind)** was to be governed by the highest form of truth. This word is still used colloquially today and is applied to those who display a sharp intuitive grasp of everyday problems.

A TERRIBLE COMBINATION

★ Very often, the boundaries between two distinct forms of human life become confused: PHILOSOPHERS BEGIN TO MEDDLE IN POLITICS AND POLITICIANS BEGIN TO USE PHILOSOPHICAL ARGUMENTS TO JUSTIFY THEIR DECISIONS. As a consequence, philosophy becomes embroiled in some **very nasty politics**.

with other people doing the hard work there was plenty of time for idle speculation

CORRUPTION BEGINS

* Athenian culture was thus responsible for a corruption of the philosophical enterprise. Philosophers, rather than challenging existing ways of looking at things, increasingly began to set themselves up as businessmen and defenders of authority. Fifth-century B.C.

enter the spiv

Athens witnessed the emergence of authoritarian philosophers like Plato who tried to use the power of philosophy to defend existing power relations in Greek society. There were also **"spiv philosophers,"** the **Sophists**, who sold their skills in logic to the highest bidder. THIS WAS A WORLD FAR REMOVED FROM THE UNTAINTED PHILOSOPHICAL CULTURE OF THE PRE-SOCRATICS.

Pericles

The most famous Athenian leader of this time was Pericles (c.495–c.429 B.C.), who waged war against Athens' archenemy Sparta. Interestingly, he hired the philosopher Anaxagoras as an advisor. Anaxagoras denied atomic metaphysics and claimed that the cosmos was governed by a great cosmic mind (**nous**). His involvement in politics led to his exile from Athens after a prosecution for "impiety," a catch-all offense especially reserved for those who had simply got too big for their boots.

I blame the Greeks

A PURE CURIOSITY

✱ Though we cannot be entirely certain about the intentions and integrity of the pre-Socratic philosophers, it is probably wise to remain charitable about their philosophical intentions. It seems clear that they "opened up" the closed and hierarchical pagan world and developed a way of thinking that was based on feelings of "wonderment" and "astonishment" at the world that surrounded them.

curiosity killed the cat

finding keys to fit

BITS AND PIECES

No complete work by any of the pre-Socratic philosophers has survived. Parmenides' poem about the goddess is the longest work left to us. Pre-Socratic ideas have been reconstructed from fragments of texts and later quotations.

ONE FOR ALL AND ALL FOR ONE

✱ This **opening up of the world** was also something of an act of POLITICAL EMANCIPATION, too. Pagan cultures were largely under the control of the shamans. For the **pre-Socratics** the world was open to interpretation by all, and each individual was alone with their freedom to make sense of "it."

✱ **The pre-Socratics did not guard their ideas jealously—others could use their ideas as they wished** and there was no sense that one philosopher's view was any more true than any other philosopher's view. There were no power struggles (at least as far as we know) between the different philosophical schools.

THE FALL FROM GRACE

* The emergence of Athenian philosophy represents the end of philosophy's innocent childhood. In fifth-century B.C. Athens, philosophy became worldly and so fell from its position of pre-Socratic grace. As we shall see in the next chapter, philosophy now gets down to business and, as such, becomes more powerful but less and less philosophical. This is where the philistines and the technocrats enter the story and try to hijack philosophy for their own purposes.

* From now on philosophy becomes AN INCREASINGLY INSTITUTIONALIZED ACTIVITY which was widely perceived to have an EDUCATIONAL ROLE in Athenian society.

philosophy lost its innocence...

AN ART FORM

Pre-Socratic philosophy was like an art. It used poetic forms to convey its meanings and tried to find gentle ways to apprehend the world that captured not just the structure of the world, but its fundamental beauty and mystery.

I'm just showing the fundamental beauty of the world

the pre-Socratics were the artists of philosophy

CHAPTER 2

TRUTH AND OPINION

* The philosophy of imperial Athens represents a turning point in the history of philosophy. It was here that the critical three-way split in the nature of human questioning discussed in the introduction emerged, a split that signified a decisive shift in the way Western culture was subsequently to value the nature of human inquiry.

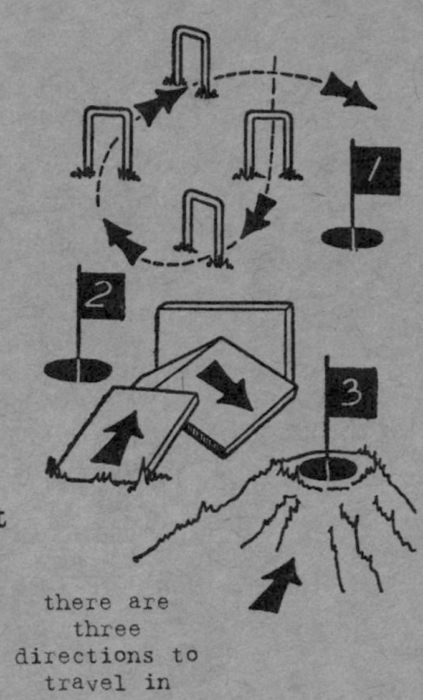

there are three directions to travel in

what shall I be when I grow up, mom?

THREE TYPES

* The Athenians were responsible for dividing the inquiring universe into three types of question and three types of questioner. I have called them the philosopher, the technocrat, and the philistine. Athenian culture laid the cultural foundations for the development of European modernity. IT WAS THE ATHENIANS WHO INSTITUTED MODES OF THINKING AND QUESTIONING THAT DISPLAY STRONG AFFINITIES WITH OUR MORE MODERN HABITS. Why was this? How did this happen?

A DEN OF INIQUITY

In much of the literature of fifth-century B.C. Athens, the city is represented as a seething cauldron of wickedness, moral degeneracy, and political intrigue.

POWERFUL ATHENS

* We need to look at the social and cultural conditions out of which this recognizably modern sensibility arose. Athens at this time was very much like our

own society in that it was undergoing a rapid and extensive social transformation.

* This transformation took place at such speed that it made the detached contemplation of the pre-Socratics seem like a quaint anachronism. Imperial Athens had grown wealthy on the back of its colonial exploits. It was the arrogance and greed that followed in the wake of this affluence that lay at the root of a cultural evil that was to prove, in the end, philosophy's undoing.

there's gold in them there hills

* In fifth-century B.C. Athens we can witness the historical birth of the **cult of reason** that was to prove influential in founding the modern technocratic world-order some 2,000 years later. It is at this point that certain key thinkers emerged who claimed that true knowledge was not speculative in nature but ought to be grounded in **"rationality."**

KEY WORDS

MODERNITY:
the modern world as experienced by Europeans, Japanese, and North Americans—a world that is now increasingly global in scope

REASON:
a cool and detached attitude to the world that attempts to understand the world in terms of abstract and universally valid principles

RATIONALITY:
any method that is guided by reason

money money money

the root of all evil grew in Athenian society

A CHANGING CLIMATE

* As Athens became a significant economic and military power, it developed a highly sophisticated form of civic administration. The older religious and newer democratic forms of political authority coexisted uneasily. This tension between a progressive democratic faction and a conservative aristocratic coalition proved to be culturally corrosive for many cherished Athenian traditions.

THE QUEST FOR POWER AND KNOWLEDGE

* The older Athenian culture was fragmenting, and new political groupings were emerging out of AN INCREASINGLY LIBERTARIAN AND COSMOPOLITAN POLITICAL CLIMATE.

* The new freedoms that colonial prosperity had delivered to the majority of the indigenous male Athenian population had allowed a critical philosophical spirit to become fashionably popular. The demand for "philosophical knowledge" grew, and prominent members of the Athenian political establishment and their ambitious sons saw that the ideas and methods of the philosophers, could, in

the right hands, be used as powerful political weapons. Political leaders hired philosophers as special advisers, and philosophy began to turn away from cosmic wonder and became instead intoxicated by power.

Euripides was sent into exile for his love of freedom

EURIPIDES

In the writings of the Athenian playwright Euripides, Athens is represented as a "glorious," divine city that champions the values of freedom and beauty. Unfortunately, this did not stop him from being ridiculed by his fellow Athenians and forced into exile in Macedonia.

when did philosophy lose its way?

* At this time Athens was a self-proclaimed democracy where political officers were elected by lot. **However, only Athenian men were allowed to take positions of political responsibility; women and slaves (of which there were many) were barred from taking part in the political life of the city.** So although Athens perceived itself as a beacon of political freedom, this was not how the city was perceived by many other Greek cities. For many, both inside and outside Athens, the city was seen as ruthless and decadent.

money is power

get ready for a significant social upheaval

THE MIGHTY COLONIALS

* This was an age of social upheaval in the Greek world. The Greeks had collectively managed to stave off the threat of Persian invasion, only to begin a bitter civil war among themselves. This was the time of the Peloponnesian War: Athens was engaged in a bitter military conflict with Sparta, a conservative military society that was, symbolically, the cultural antithesis of "democratic" Athens.

Athenian soldier

THE SPARTANS

* Sparta was a closed and self-sufficient culture whose rulers had none of the imperial ambitions of the Athenian rulers; rather they saw themselves as protectors of those parts of the Greek world that were intent on resisting Athenian imperial expansion. In this climate of political crisis and social change, the Athenian rulers turned away from their gods and **looked toward philosophy for assistance.**

actually, it's not in the lap of the gods— ask that philosopher guy

KEY WORDS

SOPHIST: itinerant philosophers who taught people rhetoric for money

RHETORIC: the art of using language to persuade others

RELATIVISM: the idea that all truths are relative to the interests of particular people at particular times; there are no absolute truths or values

SOPHISTS AS PHILISTINES

★ However, as the philosophical market expanded, some rather UNSCRUPULOUS CHARACTERS decided that significant profits were there to be made in the burgeoning "philosophy business." These people, who taught their pseudophilosophy under the name of **the sophists**, saw that there was money-making potential in the types of argument that philosophy was just beginning to develop. The methods for systematically organizing ideas that had been used by the Ionians and the Eleatics as ways of justifying the new metaphysics were now seen as tools to persuade the Athenian masses, to bewitch them into believing what was deemed politically expedient.

★ The sophists taught the values that have been commonplace in **philistine** cultures ever since: *that one's only true interest is self-interest, that there is no such thing as truth but only matters of taste and opinion, and that intelligent people should not wonder about the world, but should, instead, attempt to persuade and manipulate others to their own advantage.* The sophists were hence relativists who taught rhetoric to wealthy young Athenians, who by all accounts charged exorbitant prices for their "skills."

Sophistry sucks

The widespread unpopularity of the sophists among large sections of the Athenian political hierarchy has had the lasting effect of making the term "sophist" a term of abuse to this day.

philosophy doesn't come cheap

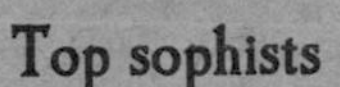

Top sophists

Foremost among the sophists were Protagoras (c.491–421 B.C.) and Gorgias (c.485–c.380 B.C.), but there were many others of lesser stature. All were itinerant teachers, most of whom arrived from the Athenian colonies in search of an easy drachma.

INTRODUCING SOCRATES

★ It was out of such unstable cultural conditions that there emerged perhaps the most significant philosopher of all time, Socrates (469-399 B.C.). All we know about his philosophy comes from the writings of his pupil Plato (c.427-347 B.C.), who, cynically, used the character of Socrates as a vehicle for his own philosophical views. So there is much debate about what Socrates was really like. We can, however, make some intelligent guesses.

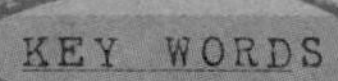

KEY WORDS

AKRASIA: lack of self-knowledge and understanding; self-deception

ELENCHUS: argumentative method that searches for the contradictions inherent in our beliefs

APORIA: state of confusion when an individual is forced to concede that his or her views are self-contradictory

it's all my own work

Plato paints a picture of Socrates

PLATO'S PORTRAIT OF SOCRATES

★ **Plato's** early writings contain no mention of the philosophical views that were to make Plato a <u>FAMOUS PHILOSOPHER</u> in his own right. It is probably safe to assume, therefore, that these early writings offer the least biased account of the ideas of **Socrates**. Thus, we can feel safe that these texts give us a reasonably accurate picture of Socrates.

Socrates

★ In these texts Socrates is represented as an arch **antisophist**, concerned about the effect that the sophists will have on the mental habits of the Athenian youth. He attempts to preserve something of the original spirit of philosophy against the sophists' spurious pseudophilosophies. However, Socrates never puts forward any philosophy of his own and seems content to accept that he is a simple and ignorant man who wonders why it is that he (and everybody else) seems to suffer from a lack of true knowledge (**akrasia**).

SOCRATES CONFUSES THE PHILISTINES

★ Socrates produced his own distinctive philosophical method that was used to expose the limitations of the sophists' new philosophies of philistinism. This method was called **elenchus** (meaning refutation) and it can be clearly seen in the two works that Plato dedicated to the ideas of the sophists. These were entitled, appropriately enough, *Protagoras* and *Gorgias*, after the two foremost sophists of the time.

★ ELENCHUS WAS A WAY OF QUESTIONING SOMEONE SO AS TO REVEAL THE CONTRADICTIONS IN THEIR STATEMENTS. The Socratic method was thus designed to produce a state of confusion (**aporia**) in those philistines who tried to define the nature of things in superficial and simple-minded ways.

ELENCHUS

Elenchus works something like this. Suppose a philistine says that he knows the true nature of the good life and boldly states that we all ought to accumulate as much money as we possibly can. Socrates would then try to show that the philistine believed in other values that conflicted with this, say beliefs about the importance of love and respect. Socrates would then retort that the philistine did not really understand the nature of the good life and, though he or she professed knowledge on this subject, they were really ignorant about such matters.

PHILOSOPHICAL LIFE

Socrates' legendary status is not simply the result of the fact that he was cruelly sentenced to death by the philistine-led Athenian government of the time. No, his philosophical fame is due to the fact that he lived a truly **philosophical life**: a life in which it is hard for the historian to tell where Socrates' deeds end and his philosophical ideas begin.

what is virtue anyway?

SOCRATES

★ Socrates was the first moral philosopher explicitly to ask the question, "What is virtue?" Concerns about justice and the nature of the good life were Socrates' central philosophical preoccupation. Although he wrote nothing himself, it is widely agreed that Socrates believed that virtue lay in having knowledge, especially self-knowledge.

QUESTIONS ARE GOOD

★ Socrates' ethics can be summed up in the phrase **"the unexamined life is not worth living."** Hence, for Socrates, questions are good and the good life begins with wonder. However, such an apparently benign and simple idea proved to be socially subversive when espoused by the philosophically pure (if politically naive) Socrates.

SOCRATES ANNOYS THE MASSES

★ Socrates was fond of walking around the Athenian marketplace and quizzing people about what they knew about themselves. He had probably acquired this habit because the source of magical authority of the time, the Delphic oracle (a kind of Greek-speaking magical well), had apparently pronounced that Socrates was the wisest of all men.

* The maxim inscribed above the oracle was "Know thyself," and Socrates was probably so flattered by all this attention from the divine oracle that he tried to turn this magical motto into a personal ethical principle. He decided to see just how well the Athenian masses lived up to his own high ethical expectations.

* To this end, Socrates would ask, say, a blacksmith, how he did his job. The blacksmith would usually reply something like, "How do I know? I just do it." Rather than leave the poor man alone to get on with his work, Socrates would then exclaim that the blacksmith was ignorant about himself and so lacking in fundamental virtue.

* This may well have been true, but there are ways of saying things. Socrates' concern for principles did not leave much room for the weaknesses of others. This resulted in most people seeing him as an irritating pain in the neck, and this clearly did not do him any favors at his **trial,** where there were very few people willing to defend him.

how are your ethical principles?

Socrates could be very annoying

The Trial

Socrates' constant questioning eventually led him to being charged with "impiety." Though, by all accounts, very few Athenians wanted Socrates put to death for this charge; all they really wanted was some kind of an apology. However, Socrates' stubborn refusal at his trial to accept any blame whatsoever turned the majority of the Athenian masses (hoi polloi) against him.

A RECOGNIZABLE PHILOSOPHER

* Socrates, however, never claimed wisdom for himself. In fact, he categorically stated that he was as ignorant about himself as everybody else was about their own selves. He just wanted to point out this general lack of self-insight so that people could do something about it and look at their own thoughts and behavior in a deeper and more significant way. Socrates was thus the first philosopher explicitly to value reflective forms of thinking. He can therefore be viewed as the first person easily recognizable as a philosopher.

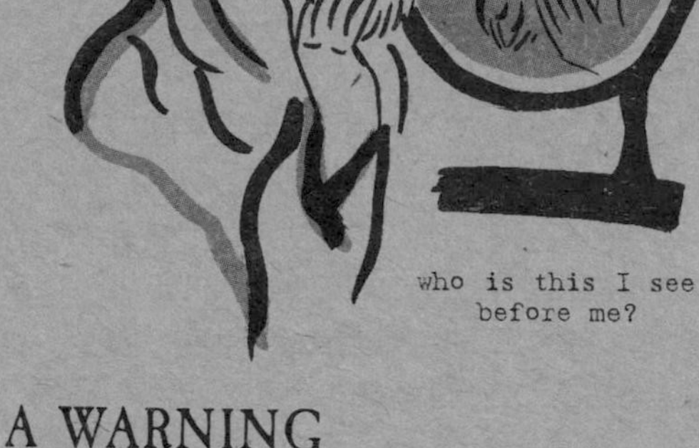

who is this I see before me?

KNOW THYSELF

Perhaps the best criticism of Socratic thought was made by **Diogenes Laertius** in his *Lives of the Philosophers* written some 700 years after Socrates' death. He writes an account of the life of Socrates, in which Socrates constantly advises the young to stare into a mirror so that they can see their beauty more clearly and remedy their ugliness.

A WARNING AGAINST NARCISSISM

* However, it would be wrong to see Socrates as a PHILOSOPHICAL MESSIAH, and his philosophy, if taken too literally, can lead to an overinflated and arrogant view of the self. For Socrates, self-knowledge can only come about through examining yourself in the mirror of self-consciousness. But, as we know, those who stare too long in the mirror can

become sick with self-obsession, as the ancient Greek myth of **Narcissus** recounts *(this is the story of a boy who fell in love with his own reflection and as a result turned into a flower).*

★ To some extent, this was true of Socrates, and the moral of his life and death should be that no matter how much virtue is reflected back at you, you should never let it go to your head.

flattery is safe as long as you don't inhale it

SOCRATES THE PHILOSOPHER'S HERO

★ However, THESE FAULTS ARE TRIVIAL WHEN COMPARED TO HIS OBVIOUS VIRTUES. Not only did Socrates keep wonder as the emotional source behind the philosophical quest for wisdom, but he also became something of role model for all subsequent philosophers. Socrates chose the free life of individual speculative reflection instead of the deceptive and manipulative life of sophistry. He chose to end his life rather than go back on what he believed was right. As he died, freely, quickly, and with justice on his side, he showed that philosophy is more than just a whimsical flight of fancy.

Oh Socrates— he's such a hero

A BRAVE DEATH

Socrates was made a scapegoat partly responsible for the collapse of the Athenian empire. The Athenian government found him guilty of corrupting the youth—because he told them to believe in themselves rather than the old gods—and sentenced him to death. Socrates would not apologize for what he had done and offered to do the job for the Athenian government: he committed suicide by drinking hemlock.

THE DEFENDER OF PHILOSOPHY

Aristophanes poked fun at Socrates in his play the clouds

★ The sophists, as we have seen, were the first to develop a worldly philosophy that was grounded in the everyday common sense of the time. The Socratic method, by unmasking the frailty at the heart of attempts to produce a common-sense understanding of the world, kept the window of philosophical speculation open.

Socrates—the defender of philosophy

A MODEL CITIZEN

Socrates was a model Athenian citizen. We know from various other commentators that he had fought in the Athenian army and had been commended for bravery.

BACK TO TRADITION

★ Socrates can thus be seen as a **defender of philosophical virtues** against a powerful cultural philistinism. However, the **Athenian philistines'** power was short-lived. THE WARLIKE AND CONSERVATIVE SPARTANS WON THE PELOPONNESIAN WAR AND IMPOSED THEIR OWN AUTHORITY ON DEFEATED ATHENS. When some kind of self-rule was restored, the recriminations started.

★ The Athenians believed that they had lost because they had neglected their gods and lost touch with traditional sources of authority. *Those who had questioned authority were made the scapegoats for Athens' military defeat, and the old ruling class began constructing a new political order based on more traditional values.*

PLATO'S SOCIAL SOLUTION

★ AFTER SOCRATES CAME PLATO. **Plato** was the son of a wealthy Athenian aristocrat and a PUPIL OF SOCRATES. He attended the trial of Socrates in 399 B.C. and was so horrified that such a virtuous man should be condemned to death that he wrote a defense of Socrates known as **The Apology**.

★ In this and later works, Plato blamed the democrats for the injustice of Socrates' death. He criticized democracy for allowing an irrational mob, driven by base and uncivilized passions, to rule the city.

★ *Plato thought that the only solution to the* **chaos of democracy** *was to use philosophy to construct a perfectly ordered society in which everybody knew their place and accepted it unquestioningly.*

★ In the hands of Plato, Socrates becomes the spokesperson for **Plato's own authoritarian philosophy**. In Plato's middle and later writings, Socrates becomes more than simply a thorn in the sophists' side—he begins to formulate metaphysical ideas in his own right, ideas that were really Plato's own.

ARISTOPHANES

Socrates was often mistaken for a sophist, and the playwright Aristophanes (c.448-388 B.C.) lampooned both Socrates and the sophists as silly pedants in his satirical play **The Clouds**. But Socrates was no sophist and was trying to prevent philosophy from becoming embroiled in the cynical culture of the Athenian marketplace (**agora**).

Plato's plan: order through acceptance

SOCRATES IN PLATO'S HANDS

eat, stand around, trot, neigh, gallop, sweat, eat

★ In Plato's later works, Socrates is made to argue that any attempt to define the property associated with something, for example, "good," in terms of something else, for example, having lots of money, leads to confusion (aporia). Hence, goodness must exist independently for the term to have any meaning at all. For Plato, each substantive word, like, say, horse, refers to an essential property of the thing named—"horseness."

am I a horse or a cow?

HORSENESS

It is only because we know what "horseness" is—the eternal essence possessed by all horses—that we are capable of recognizing any particular horse as a horse. Particular horses are said to participate in the form of a horse, and this is what makes them horses as opposed to, say, cows.

THE ESSENCE OF THINGS

★ Why did Plato believe that every existing object or property contains such an underlying **essence**? For Plato, the world of appearance was not a reliable source of knowledge and, like Parmenides, he looked for the source of true knowledge in an unchanging and eternal realm of being. He saw this realm of being as populated with what he called **forms**, and each form was a representation of the underlying essence of a property or thing.

yes madame, I have got essence of horse today

★ Every object or property in the realm of appearances, like a horse, for example, has an ideal version associated with it in the eternal realm of being. It is the fact that certain humans can apprehend these ideal types of objects that makes **knowledge** of everyday objects possible at all.

what about the eternal realm of being?

it's very ducky therefore it must be a duck

what is it?

RECOGNIZING THINGS

★ *For Plato, then (as told through his mouthpiece Socrates), the basic problem of philosophy changes from a metaphysical problem, "What is it?" to the epistemological problem, "How can we know about it?"* For Plato, it is only because we know the form of a thing—that is, the eternal, transcendental, and universal essence of that thing—that we can recognize that particular thing as it actually is.

KEY WORDS

FORMS:
the eternal timeless underlying structure of a particular thing that defines the nature of that thing. For example, the true reality of a chair, is not the way it appears to ordinary mortals but is its ideal representation in the world of forms.

what are they?

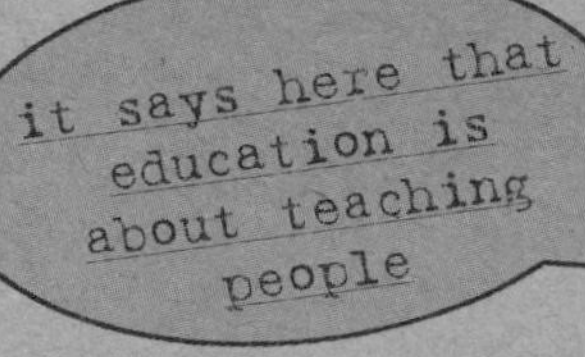

THE REALM OF FORMS

* Plato drew some important social and cultural conclusions from these epistemological and metaphysical doctrines. Firstly, according to Plato, education should be about teaching people to access the eternal realm of the forms and not about 'how to win friends and influence people' as the sophists advocated.

let me out, I've got things to do

LIFE BEFORE BIRTH

* For Plato, EVERYBODY HAD ACCESS TO THIS REALM BEFORE THEY WERE BORN, but after birth had forgotten about this eternal realm of idealized objects and properties and got on with more mundane matters. For Plato, the task of education was to help people to recollect what they tacitly knew but had somehow forgotten. It was about **"drawing knowledge out"** from the hidden depths of the psyche rather than simply **"putting knowledge in."**

A TECHNOCRAT

The fact that Plato believed that "truth" should be placed in the care of experts and that the vast majority of humans were too vile and dumb to appreciate it makes Plato the first technocratic "philosopher."

THE PHILOSOPHER'S ROLE

* Plato's philosophy seems innocent enough at first glance, but a closer reading reveals some strong authoritarian undercurrents. These can easily be seen in Plato's famous allegory of **the cave** in his most significant work, *The Republic*. In this work, Plato depicts the philosophical

situation of common humanity as being rather like people chained to a cave wall, with the sunlit entrance behind them. All that people can see are the shadows cast on the wall by the mysterious unseen things moving outside the cave. Most people, in their ignorance, take these shadows to be reality. It is the role of the philosopher to liberate them from their shadowy existence and escort them into the bright noon of knowledge and up into the true and eternal realm of being.

you need liberation

listen to me: I know best

★ It is only because the philosopher already possesses this **superior knowledge** that it is possible to ESCAPE THE SHADOW WORLD OF EVERYDAY LIFE. For Plato, it is the **philosopher who knows best**; it is only those sensitive enough to apprehend the eternal forms from the shadows of appearance who are fit to guide the mass of humanity into the illumination of eternal truth.

PLATO'S REPUBLIC

★ In *The Republic*, Plato puts forward his theory of the nature of the human soul, and he uses this theory to build a model of what is, in his opinion, **the ideal state**.

The Soul

For Plato the human soul consists of three independent and antagonistic parts: the "reasoning part," "the spirited part," and "the appetitive part." The highest and most valued part of the soul for Plato was the "reasoning part," or intellect, for it was only this part that was capable of apprehending the absolute truth of the eternal world of forms. The other parts of the soul were seen as morally less significant than the intellect in that they were seen to be more chaotic and unruly.

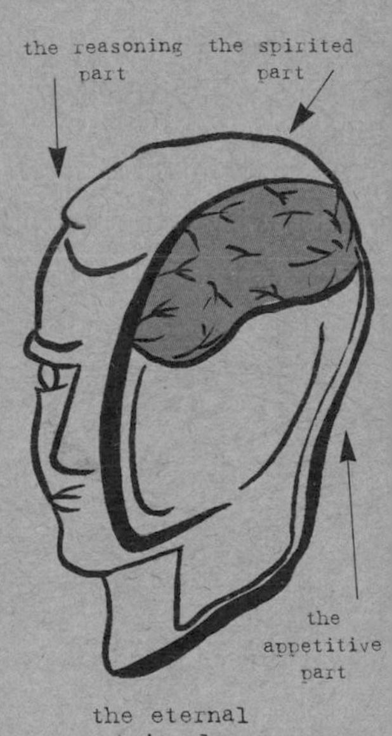

the eternal triangle

join Plato's academy

THE HIERARCHICAL IDEAL

* Plato thinks that his ideal state should be organized along the same lines as the soul. Society should be split into three distinct classes, with the expert philosophers at the top of the social hierarchy, a military class of warriors in the middle, and the passionate and unruly masses at the bottom. Those at the bottom would work as producers of goods and services for those above, but would be protected by the knowledge and courage of those above them.

THE ACADEMY

Plato's Academy provided the model for all subsequent schools; even present-day schools are, to some extent, organized according to Platonic principles.

BANISHING THE POETS

* Most importantly, there is no room for **the poets** in Plato's ideal republic. The poets, with their taste for fantastic imaginings, pose a threat to the rational philosophical order of Plato's IDEAL CITY-STATE.

* According to Plato, then, they must necessarily be **banished from the city** if any kind of social order is to survive.

* *It could be said that one can see Platonic political philosophy at work in modern societies. This is a key question to which we will return later on.*

and you can get lost!

PLATO'S PUPILS

★ **There is a certain affinity, then, between Plato's epistemology and his politics.** Plato's philosophy claims that THERE IS AN ETERNAL TRUTH-REALM ONLY ACCESSIBLE TO THE INITIATED FEW. So if we wish to organize society according to truthful principles and prevent society from being at the whim of a deceiving popular opinion, it should be ruled by the philosopher kings.

★ For Plato there is only one metaphysical truth—**his**—and only one way of knowing it—**by becoming his pupil**. So that his gospel would live after his death, Plato set up his own school, **the Academy**. It was dedicated to teaching the "brightest" young Greek men techniques for apprehending the way to the truth. *Here we can see the arrival of the "experts" who know what the rest of us should do.*

ARISTOTLE'S VIEW OF NATURE

★ The CONVERSION OF PHILOSOPHY INTO A JUSTIFICATION FOR TECHNOCRACY was finally completed with the work of Plato's pupil **Aristotle**.

★ Aristotle removed the last vestiges of wonder from classical Platonism. He argued that forms did not exist in some transcendent, ethereal realm but were immanent in Nature. HIS WAS THE FIRST SYSTEMATIC ATTEMPT TO CLASSIFY AND CODIFY NATURE.

Plato's legacy was the Academy

Aristotle

Aristotle was born in 384 B.C. in Macedonia. His father was a well-connected local doctor and friend and personal physician to the king. Aristotle went to study under Plato at the Athenian Academy and then later returned to Macedonia as personal tutor to the teenage Alexander the Great (356–323 B.C.), the future mad, despotic, and tyrannical conqueror of vast tracts of southern Europe, north Africa, and what is now the Middle East. Aristotle's influence on the moral and social development of the great Alexander can only be surmised.

will that be all?

THE BIRTH OF LOGIC

★ With Aristotle, philosophy begins its technocratic role as servant and guardian to technical science in earnest. Aristotle's philosophy can therefore be seen as a foundational precursor to modern biological sciences. Furthermore, Aristotle was the first philosopher to attempt to classify arguments into types, distinguishing between valid and invalid arguments. He thus tried to formulate technical rules of argument and was the founder of the science of argument: logic.

philosophy: the hors d'oeuvres

A PUBLISHER PLAYS HIS PART

★ **Aristotle's** publisher was the first to make the distinction between physics and metaphysics. After he had written his work on physics, he wrote another work that developed further some of the philosophical issues raised in the previous work. Unfortunately, he didn't provide a title, and his publisher suggested that "METAPHYSICS"—meaning, "after physics"—seemed the most appropriate term. It stuck, and philosophers have been **lumbered** with this most misleading of philosophical terms ever since.

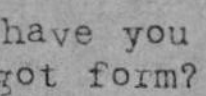

have you got form?

★ For Aristotle, **physics deals with the explanation of the natural world** while **metaphysics deals with "being as such."** For Aristotle, "being as such," or "it," can be understood in terms of **ten categories**: SUBSTANCE, QUANTITY, QUALITY, RELATION, PLACE, TIME, POSITION, STATE, ACTION, AND AFFECTION. The most basic of these categories is **substance**, because it represents the fixed, underlying essence of any particular thing. Substance for Aristotle consists of **form** and **matter**, the former giving determinate shape to indeterminate material.

FULFILLING YOUR POTENTIAL

★ Another important distinction in Aristotle's metaphysics is that between **actuality** and **potentiality**. *For Aristotle, the dynamism inherent in the cosmos exists because everything contains within itself the potential to become what it is finally meant to be.* So, for example, acorns are potential trees, children potential adults, and politicians potential thieves. What remains constant throughout the development of any particular thing is its substance and ITS DEVELOPMENT IS GOVERNED BY ITS FORM. In this respect, Aristotle remained Plato's pupil, and both can be seen as the founding fathers of technocratic thought.

God intervenes

We are now going to begin a chapter in philosophy's history when it is driven underground by a new powerful religious force, Christianity. With the emergence of Christianity, all philosophical speculation becomes oriented toward proving the existence of the Judeo-Christian God and other assorted religious beliefs. Philosophy becomes the foundational arm of theology. Was this a case of out of the frying pan into the fire?

God puts his two cents in

THE STOICS AND THE SKEPTICS

the Stoics met under an Athenian portico

* Before we move on from Greece to the Romans and the Christians, three further schools of philosophy deserve to be mentioned. Firstly there were the Stoics. This was a philosophical school founded in Athens by Zeno of Citium at the end of the fourth century B.C. This school's philosophy was known as stoicism and was so-called because the Stoics regularly gave lessons in a porch (the Greek word for porch was "stoa") known as the "Painted Portico."

UNDER THE PORCH

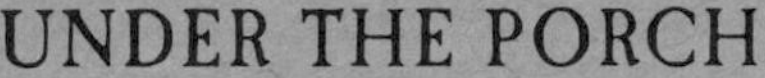

* They taught that the most important philosophical questions were ETHICAL ONES and that the good life was about quietly **"getting on with it"** and not wallowing in self-pity when life gets tough. They did, however, keep the true spirit of philosophy alive, and they managed to maintain a **sense of wonder** about the cosmos and our place in it at a time when the cynicism of **Diogenes** was becoming increasingly popular. The Stoic philosophical vision was ESSENTIALLY ETHICAL: that we are

STOICISM SPREADS

The ideas of the Stoics became increasingly popular and their influence spread from Greece to Rome. Seneca (5 B.C. –A.D. 65), the Roman adviser to the mad emperor Nero (A.D. 37–68), is said to have been impressed by the Stoic idea that excessive passion was evil. It is a pity that he couldn't persuade his boss that this was the case.

Stoics thought that getting on with it was the key to a good life

all citizens of the cosmos (**cosmopolitanis**) and that we all have a duty to each other.

* However, we must accept that there is only so much we can do in a cosmos that is, by its very nature, out of our control. For the Stoic, the wise and virtuous person remains calm in the face of an uncertain and hostile world and so the expression "to be stoical" has become an expression that is often used to refer to those who seem at ease with themselves in the face of adversity.

the Stoics didn't lose their sense of wonder

DON'T ASK

* At around the same time, **Pyrrho** was advocating a philosophy known as SKEPTICISM. This philosophy, which has been adored by philistines ever since, claimed that the only way to live a virtuous life was to dispense with philosophy altogether and avoid asking such questions, since there weren't any answers to them.

KEY WORDS

STOIC:
a person who advocates an ethic of resilience in the face of adversity; a believer in liberal cosmopolitan politics

CYNIC:
a person who believes in individual self-sufficiency and withdrawal from a "corrupt world"

SKEPTIC:
a person who claims that is impossible ever to arrive at knowledge or truth

Nihilism

The best thing to do, the skeptics thought, was to believe in nothing, to give nothing away, and to feel as little emotion as possible. You could say they adopted philosophical views that displayed a noticeable similarity to those of some modern-day, right-wing politicians.

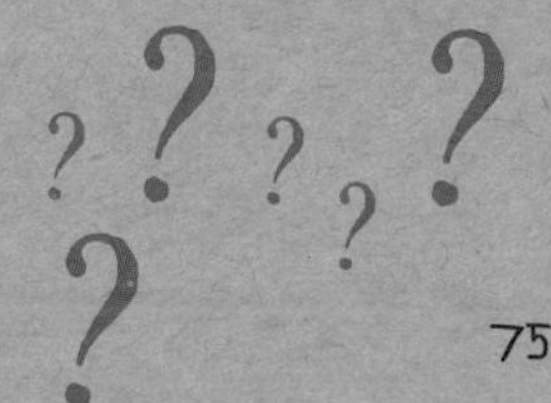

HOW TO SEE THE TRUTH

★ Toward the end of the third century B.C., Platonic ideas experienced something of a popular revival. This was largely due to Plotinus (A.D. 205-270) who thought that Plato was divine and founded his own school, Neoplatonism, which attempted to transform Platonic philosophy and Eastern mystical thought into a new mystery religion.

Plato re-examined

KEY WORDS

NEOPLATONISM: ancient mystical philosophy based on the later writings of Plato

THE ONE: incomprehensible, self-sufficient unity that emanates from the divine cosmic logos

achieving ultimate liberation

FREE THE SOUL

★ The ultimate goal of **Neoplatonic** philosophy was to LIBERATE THE SOUL, to leave the embodied world of the senses behind so that this emancipated spirit could achieve an ecstatic union with the divine **"One."** In this state, the individual lost any sense of his- or herself and identified with **"the All"** or, as it is now more commonly referred to, **God**. It was during such episodes of TRANSCENDENTAL EGO-DEATH that the truth was revealed to the newly liberated individual.

THREE IN ONE

★ Like Plato, Plotinus believed that truth existed in another realm beyond the illusory world of appearances. However, Plotinus divided this realm into three levels, the highest being the One, the second being the Spirit, and the lowest level being the Soul. True liberation could only be obtained from contemplation of the highest level and by renouncing the everyday world. Plotinus' philosophy thus represents a hybrid of religious and philosophical ideas, and his threefold metaphysical division of the eternal "One" was later to be turned into **the Father, Son, and Holy Ghost**, the metaphysical foundation for Catholic Christianity.

the Romans didn't think much of philosophy

WHEN IN ROME

★ These philosophies never achieved the significance of their Greek predecessors and Roman culture tended to view philosophical ideas as being rather like quaint collectable antiques. The ideas that were to play center stage in the dramas of Roman history were not philosophical but religious. The cultural significance of classical philosophy was trivial compared to the new religious ideas that emerged out of Palestine in the first century A.D.

Fun, Fun, Fun

Unlike Plato, Neoplatonists believed that knowledge of the truth was an enjoyable experience and nothing at all like doing geometry, as Plato had thought. In fact, Plotinus claimed that union with the divine could produce orgasmic ecstasies in those philosophically adept enough to grasp this mysterious eternal truth. It is no surprise then, that his idea became very popular among adolescent Roman boys.

JURISPRUDENCE

The only significant new thinking to emerge from Rome was **jurisprudence** (the philosophy of law). From Roman law we get the idea that law should apply to everyone, irrespective of creed or culture (**jus gentium**), and this idea was clearly a precursor to the modern idea that everyone has **rights**.

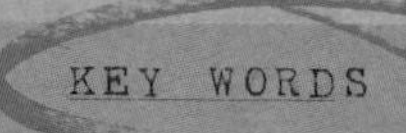

ZOROASTRIANISM: ancient Persian religion that viewed the universe as an eternal struggle between forces of light and darkness

JUDAISM: the religion of the Jewish people, conceived largely in captivity, that hopes for salvation from a future messiah

HEDONISM: the idea that pleasure is the ultimate good

A Popular Belief

Zoroastrianism still has many adherents today. The late pop-star Freddie Mercury is claimed to have been a follower of the religion. It has profoundly influenced the history of philosophy; the German philosopher Nietzsche is said to have been sympathetic to some of its doctrines.

GOD AND THE UNIVERSE

* Alexander the Great's military campaigns were instrumental in expanding Greek cultural influence into what is now Egypt, the Middle East, and out into India. Almost inevitably this brought Greek culture into contact with many other cultures that adhered to very different religious and philosophical traditions. Alexander was perceived to be a god incarnate by many of the vanquished in the new colonies.

RECIPROCAL INFLUENCES

* But the colonized also influenced the colonizers, and the two most important cultural imports to the classical world of antiquity were **Zoroastrianism** (from Persia) and **Judaism** (from Palestine).

* The long-term effect of these ways of thinking on the classical world was enormous, and their influence was to prove, in the end, that the classical world could not live on a simple diet of Roman "bread and circuses."

this is a bit better than old Roman bread

★ Following Alexander's death in 323 B.C., the Greek empire collapsed, and political power in the Mediterranean shifted from the east to the west, from Greece to Rome. In 146 B.C., Greece became a Roman colony and Rome was about to begin the cultural dominion over Europe and beyond that was to last until the barbarian invasions some 500 years later.

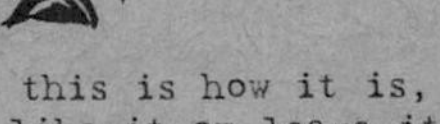

this is how it is, like it or leave it

LAW AND POLITICS RULE

★ Underneath the absolute power of the Roman emperor (who by the first century A.D. was seen by the **plebeian** masses as a god) was a **patrician** class of career politicians. They presided over an extensive bureaucracy that governed by means of a constitutional **law** (a Roman invention), supported by a well-organized **professional army**. Roman society can thus be viewed as a hybrid of paganism and technocracy that had no use for the aimless speculations of the philosophers.

★ The only Roman philosopher of note was **Lucretius** (98–55 B.C.). He was a follower of the Greek philosopher **Epicurus** (341–270 B.C.). Like Epicurus, Lucretius was an **ethical hedonist,** but in his book *De Rerum Natura* he philosophized with true Roman spirit and contemplated the laws of the universe.

IMPERIUM

With Roman rule the older, more traditional, types of authority were restored. Paganism became the official state-sponsored religion and imperial monarchy the only form of legitimate government.

Roman philosophy was not the only way

THE GOSPEL TRUTH

there was quite a struggle between sects

★ Palestine's status as a Roman colony was a source of some resentment among certain members of the many radical Jewish sects that existed at this time. Palestine was also the place where Greek, Judaic, and Persian philosophies met each other, and from this cultural melting pot there appeared a new religion that was to become the foundation of medieval Europe—Christianity.

God started everything

Gnosticism

Gnosticism says that the universe was created by a wicked God. According to the Gnostics, Yahweh, the god of the Jews, was a nefarious villain who created the universe out of spite to trap the human spirit in a vile material body. Hence, the Gnostics believed that **matter**, Yahweh's creation, was evil.

JESUS AS A RADICAL JEW

★ Although we know little about the life of the historical Jesus, Christianity's founder, it is now widely agreed that his ideas were similar to those expressed in the writings of the groups of radical Jews who had formed religious communities on the banks of the Dead Sea. These Jewish thinkers believed in the basic tenet of orthodox Judaism, that the world had been created by a single God, but they had also been influenced by a variety of Persian Zoroastrianism that has become known as **Gnosticism**.

Jesus the radical

GNOSTIC THOUGHT

* The true God, according to the Gnostics, was not of this world and was yet to make his appearance. For Gnostics then, there was not one God, but two: one evil and the other one good. Hence, they opposed **monotheism** (the idea that there is only one God), expressed in Yahweh's command to "WORSHIP NO OTHER GOD BUT ME." For the Gnostics, the true and good God was completely divorced from material reality and thus impossible to know even in the most speculative way. *True reality was to be found in the life of the spirit that could only be lived, not speculated about.*

* After Jesus' crucifixion, many claimed that he was the Messiah sent by the good God (who has been given the name "Abraxas" by subsequent Gnostics such as the twentieth-century German novelist **Herman Hesse**). This message was carried forward by the Roman tent-maker later to be canonized, Paul.

WAITING FOR THE MESSIAH

The good life for the Gnostics meant denying the pleasures of the evil flesh and waiting for the true Messiah to lead them into the kingdom of God. This, they believed, was about to happen very soon. There was no room for philosophy in their disciplined, ascetic culture and as such they were rather like modern **Protestants**.

HISTORY REWRITTEN

* Within two centuries there were Christians all over the Roman world, most of whom believed that the truth had nothing to do with philosophy, but was revealed to us through the written Gospels of Jesus' life and teaching.

chipping away at history

Bad Boy

Augustine had, by all accounts, led something of a misspent youth by Christian standards. At the age of thirty-one he decided to convert to Christianity, the religion of his mother, and dedicated his life to saving the world from the evils of paganism and Gnosticism.

Constantine

Redemption

The only way to be redeemed from sin was to repent, and, for Augustine, it was only by accepting the divine grace of Jesus Christ that any individual could ever hope to be freed from the curse of carnal knowledge. The Christian idea that the fundamental question of human life is whether faith can save us from an awareness of sin stems from Augustinian thought.

CHRISTIANITY RISES

★ By the fourth century A.D. the so-called barbarians, especially the Huns and the many varieties of Goth, had seriously undermined the power of the Roman Empire. Prior to this, Christianity had been outlawed by the Roman state, and Christians had been viewed by the Roman administration as being more like pet food than people. But in A.D. 312 the emperor Constantine, probably in a desperate attempt to bring political stability back to Rome, converted to Christianity.

JUSTIFYING GOD

★ The growing influence of **Christianity** in the Roman world spawned a series of philosophies that had the express intention of GIVING THE CHRISTIAN FAITH A METAPHYSICAL JUSTIFICATION. The most famous of these early Christian philosophers was **Augustine Bishop of Hippo** (born in Carthage, now Algeria, in 354 B.C.). His most famous works were the *Confessions*, where he confessed the past excesses of his former sinful life, and the *City of God*, in which he was to construct the philosophical foundations of a new Catholic theology. He wrote this to provide an increasingly powerful Christian

Church with a set of justifications for constructing itself as a "Church militant," a political organization intent on eradicating both paganism and Gnostic Christian heresies.

Augustine turned over a new leaf

AUGUSTINE'S THEOLOGY

* In the *City of God* we can clearly see the influence NEOPLATONISM was to exert upon Augustine's philosophical theology. Augustine's idea of God was derived from Plato's idea of the eternal "good" and Plotinus' conception of the divine "One." **For Augustine, the one true God was the benign author of everything in the cosmos**. However, Augustine's originality was that he was the first to attempt a synthesis of Judeo-Christian religion and Platonic metaphysics, thus producing the first recognizably Christian metaphysical account of the nature of the cosmos.

Augustine

Original sin

Augustine believed that the human soul had been corrupted at the fall of Adam and all those born of flesh since had been infected by Adam's sin. As a result, he thought that all humanity was condemned to suffer pain, guilt, and finally, death for Adam's transgression.

it was all
his fault

Adam and Eve, the original sinners

THE FIGHT AGAINST EVIL

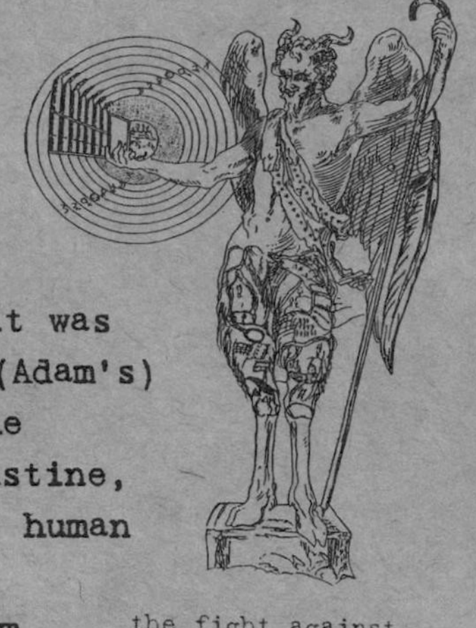

the fight against evil became important

★ Augustine believed that the cosmos was the perfect creation of a divine will and it was only as a consequence of man's (Adam's) free will that there existed the problem of evil. Evil, for Augustine, was anything overly sensual, so human sexuality was one of the main targets for his moral opprobrium.

HEAVENLY BLISS

according to Augustine, anything sensual was evil

★ Evil, according to Augustine, can only be truly overcome in the next life, where the righteous will live a perfect existence forever when they return to the **divine One** in heaven. In the meantime, the only thing that could be done on earth to fight the evil of human carnality was to build politically strong church structures that were capable of spreading the consoling words of the divine life and teachings of Jesus to the heathen masses.

★ For Augustine, the divine cosmic logos was no longer an impersonal principle, but with the birth of Jesus was made flesh. For the early Christians, then, Jesus was metaphysics transformed into a man, and the fundamental truth of the cosmos was Christ's life and teachings.

PHILOSOPHERS PERSECUTED

★ Following the decline of the western empire, the Roman Catholic Church, supported by Augustinian philosophical arguments, became the religious orthodoxy of the time. By the beginning of the sixth century A.D. many of the barbarian invaders had been converted to Catholicism, and philosophical speculation increasingly became associated with the "evils" of classical paganism. Philosophers now found themselves persecuted as non-believers alongside heretics and pagans.

I don't think much of this persecution stuff

END OF AN ERA

In 529 Plato's Academy closed. The age of the great debate between philosophers, technocrats, and philistines was now over.

BOETHIUS

The last true classical philosopher was Boethius (c.475–c.525). Boethius was imprisoned by the Italian king Theodoric for paganism and practicing black magic. In jail he wrote **The Consolations of Philosophy**, in which he rejects the truth of Christianity. He relates how the goddess Philosophia appeared to him in his cell to "direct him to true happiness." This is best captured by the maxim "a wise man's very distress is an opportunity to strengthen his wisdom." Boethius' execution in c.526 suggests that such a simple stoicism had little to say about the injustices of this world.

ISLAM DISCOVERS PHILOSOPHY

*** After the fall of the Western empire, the Roman Empire moved east to Byzantium. At around the same time, in what is now Saudi Arabia, the Arab mystic Muhammad was busy uniting the Bedouin tribes into an Arabic empire with the unifying glue of Islam.**

Islam encountered the Roman empire

eureka! I've discovered philosophy

Muhammad discovers philosophy

ARISTOTLE TRIUMPHS

* By the beginning of the eighth century A.D. the Arab armies had captured **Byzantine Syria** and **Alexandria**—famous for its library, an unrivaled center of classical learning in the late antique world. This expansion of Islam into "the West" and Islamic culture's appropriation of some of the most revered symbols of western culture was to produce some REMARKABLE CULTURAL CHANGES, not least of which was the "discovery" of classical philosophy by Islamic scholars.

* Pagan Byzantium had favored ARISTOTLE the naturalist over PLATO the mystic. **As a result, Aristotle's ideas had the most significant influence on Islamic thought.** The first Islamic Aristotelian of note was **Avicenna** (980–1037), who taught philosophy in Tehran at the end of the tenth century.

THE ARABIC PHILOSOPHERS

★ Avicenna tried to use Aristotle's ideas to prove the existence of a self-existent **necessary being**, God, who was the supreme foundation of all things. He was also famous for his claim that a thing was not identical to its essence. This rather unAristotelian thought (Aristotle thought that his categories gave us the essence of a

the famous library at Alexandria

particular thing) was later used by the **existentialists** in the philosophical motto *"existence precedes essence."*

★ The Spanish philosopher **Averroës** (1126–98) brought classical thinking back to Western culture. Averroës worshiped Aristotle as a prophet, and believed that his ideas could be used to devise purely **rational proof** of God's existence. This provoked a Muslim theologian, **Algazel**, to write *The Destruction of the Philosophers*, in which he claimed that philosophy was an evil that corrupted the soul.

MAIMONIDES

Maimonides (1135–1204) was a Jewish philosopher who acknowledged a debt to the Arabic Aristotelians. His most famous work was the *Guide for the Perplexed*, in which he attempted to harmonize the teachings of Aristotle with Judaism. He argued that neither Muhammad nor Aristotle offered us a convincing account of the truth, but that we should see the pursuit of truth as being a spiritual quest in its own right.

NEW THINKING IN CATHOLICISM

★ So, while western Europe was suffering from an excess of Christianity, the old classical debates were continuing in the Islamic world. It was only in the twelfth century, after the defeat of the Arabs by the Christians in Spain, that the philosophical issues raised by the classical thinkers of Greece and Rome came to life again in the Christian West. This led to the emergence of new philosophically driven ways of thinking in the Catholic Church, ways of thinking that have become known as scholasticism.

I find Aristotle especially interesting

IN CONTROL

The medieval Church can be seen as instituting a kind of **spiritual technocracy** that used a priestly synthesis of religion and philosophy as a means of social control (by instilling guilt in the sinners and offering hope of a better life in heaven to the righteous).

THE SCHOOLMEN

★ These philosophers were called the "SCHOOLMEN" and "scholasticism" means the "philosophy of the schoolmen."

★ The most famous of these were **Thomas Aquinas** (see pages 90–93), **William of Ockham**, and **Duns Scotus** (c.1265–1308). All three were interested in how to combine the **rationalism** of Aristotelian thought with the revealed faith of Christianity. They found Aristotle's logic and his metaphysical materialism especially interesting and they used Aristotelian philosophy to construct an entire **cosmology** that was to be the dominant conception of the world for some 450 years until the emergence of **Renaissance Humanism**.

Thomas Aquinas

THE MEDIEVAL COSMOS

* Medieval cosmology was a "world view" that understood the cosmos as an enormous material sphere that was completely filled with matter. It was also divided into two parts, the CELESTIAL and the TERRESTRIAL.

celestial's up there, and terrestrial's down here

* The celestial region was understood as being made of a perfect, incorruptible ether that was timeless and changeless. This was the realm of God and the angels.
* The terrestrial region, where human beings lived, was made of the elements: EARTH, FIRE, AIR, AND WATER. Each of these elements had its own "natural purpose" that governed its behavior.
* This view of the cosmos was to provide psychological, spiritual, and intellectual nourishment to Western culture until the sixteenth century.

THOMAS AQUINAS

★ The revival of popular interest in both the philosophical ideas of Aristotle and pagan forms of religious worship in twelfth-century Europe occurred outside the controlled and disciplinary structures of the Church. Clearly this threat to the Church's authority had to be addressed. But the Catholic Church is nothing if not adaptable, and to cope with these cultural changes, it used two methods.

KEY WORDS

SCHOLASTIC: medieval philosopher-Catholics dedicated to proving rational proofs for the revealed truths of religion

PROOF: an argument from certain and self-evident "assumptions" toward some significant, novel conclusion

the schoolmen's efforts missed the mark

CHANGES IN CATHOLICISM

★ First, the Church invented the cult of Mary to appeal to women, who had traditionally been more sympathetic to paganism. Second, the more curious clerics attempted to synthesize the Church's monotheistic theology with Aristotelian metaphysics. Aquinas, being a good Catholic boy with a taste for logic and metaphysics, dedicated himself to this course.

Thomas Aquinas

AQUINAS' WRITINGS

★ Thomas Aquinas was born in 1224 in Naples. After graduating from the university there, he joined the Dominican order (the order of preachers that was also later to become the inquisitorial order) and basically began to write and write and write. He is said to have written some eight million words, and, considering that he did this without the help of even a pencil-sharpener, we must admit that this was a heroic achievement.

★ Most of Aquinas' **eight million** words were about how to produce a RATIONAL PROOF OF GOD'S EXISTENCE. He was also concerned with producing philosophically articulate accounts of the nature of evil, human freedom, and the worth of the human soul.

★ His first major work on theology, *Summa Contra Gentiles* (*On the Truth of the Catholic Faith Against the Gentiles*), tried to defend the basic tenets of Roman Catholicism—the existence of an all-powerful, all-knowing, and benevolent God, the reality of human freedom and evil, the nature and reality of angels, etc. This work is full of detailed points on logic and intricate technical arguments that look, to the casual reader, like the worst kind of pedantic hairsplitting.

NOT A GREAT SUCCESS

Summa Contra Gentiles seems to have been intended to convert pagans and Muslims to the Catholic faith, but its difficulty and obscurity meant that it produced few converts. For this reason, the term "scholastic" has come to refer to any task that looks like a pointless academic exercise. This is probably how the pagans received Aquinas' efforts.

PROOF OF GOD'S EXISTENCE

a philosopher

* In his most famous work, the *Summa Theologica*, Aquinas offers five proofs for the existence of God based on many of Aristotle's ideas, especially his idea on the impossibility of infinite regress. This states that reasons or causes cannot go on forever; at some point a chain of reasons or causes has to cease.

AQUINAS STARTS SOMETHING BIG

The truths of reason and revelation are not easily married, not even in an all-accepting Catholic Church. The long-term effect of Aquinas' philosophy was to ignite the slow-burning fuse of secular thought within the Church; a way of thinking that was wholly **naturalist** and atheist in philosophical outlook.

MORE PROOF

* Aquinas' first proof, THE ARGUMENT FROM MOTION, argues that because there is movement, there must be a "first unmoved mover" and this is clearly God.
* The second argument, THE ARGUMENT FROM EFFICIENT CAUSES, states that since there exists in the universe an "order of efficient causes," there must exist a first efficient cause, which is God.
* The third argument, THE ARGUMENT FROM CONTINGENCY, states that in nature the existence of something is always contingent on the existence of something else. The only way we can make sense of this state of metaphysical dependency (without infinite regress), is to accept that there must exist a necessary being, that is a being, whose existence is not dependent on anything else. This is God.

YET MORE PROOF

* The fourth argument, THE ARGUMENT FROM DEGREES OF EXCELLENCE, states that because we can make distinctions between the more and the less perfect, there must exist an ultimate standard of perfection, and that is God.

* The fifth argument, THE ARGUMENT FROM DESIGN, states that everywhere in nature we can see evidence of God's intention; nature seems to be a harmonious system where everything seems to exist for some ultimate purpose. So the universe must have had a designer, and this is God.

what do you find when you lift up the stone?

* None of these proofs is convincing on its own, but together they provide a kind of rational support for the main tenets of Catholic theology. Aquinas thought they complemented the **revealed** mysteries of the Catholic faith and never intended them to supplant the revealed truths with more rational foundational truths.

KEY WORDS

NATURALISM: the idea that everything, including the human mind (or spirit) is thoroughly part of nature

INFINITE REGRESS: Aristotle's idea that a chain of causes cannot go on forever; Aquinas uses this idea to show that the beginning and the end of all causes must be a single, unchanging, godlike thing

RELIGION VS. RATIONALISM

The works of Aquinas and his associates started the erosion of the power of religious institutions that was to result in the Enlightenment. The scholastic awakening lifted the stone of religion from the heart of humanity and initiated a search for a more rational way of ordering society. But what crawled out from underneath?

A SCIENTIFIC ORDER

spinning the universal machine

* The discoveries of Copernicus and Galileo overturned the cosmology of the schoolmen and started the long process of constructing an alternative scientific cosmology. In this scheme the universe was no longer seen as a morally ordered spiritual sphere, but was understood as a mechanical machine subject only to harsh and impersonal mathematical laws. This brought about a new social order that differed from its religious ancestor in some significant ways.

Copernicus

SCIENCE AND TECHNOLOGY

* **The new world was to be governed by the "truths" of science**, truths that were based on the careful manipulation and observation of nature within a MATHEMATICAL EPISTEMOLOGICAL FRAMEWORK.

* There was to be **no place for philosophy** as we have defined it in the brave new world of scientific **modernity**. From now on, ANALYSIS, METHOD, AND TECHNIQUE WOULD BE THE NEW GODS, and the wonder and curiosity of the philosophers was to be replaced with

I think I'll bring about a new social order

a new kind of question. The question, **"What is it?"** was now subordinated to the more technical question, **"How does it work?"** So philosophy became concerned with providing the metaphysical and epistemological supports for the new secular order of **modern technocracy**.

has modern science lost its sense of wonder?

GALILEO

LOSS OF FAITH

With the scientific revolution Europeans lost their faith in religion but found new hope in the technocratic religions of science and humanism. Both of these seemed to offer more rational ways of achieving salvation.

MARKET ECONOMY

* According to most sociologists, this new secular order began in the sixteenth century with the rise of a market economy and the growth of a centralized bureaucratic state. Both of these institutions had no need for philosophical wisdom as such. WHAT THE BURGEONING STATE AND MARKET REQUIRED WAS ACCURATE INFORMATION, AND LOTS OF IT.

accurate information was needed

CHAPTER 4

THE RISE OF THE TECHNOCRATS

★ The collapse of the medieval world view was caused by a variety of different factors: the perceived corruption of the Catholic Church hierarchy, the increase in wealth and power of a new "merchant" class, and the new astronomical discoveries of Copernicus and Galileo all played their part in undermining the religious and metaphysical foundations of Christian Europe.

KEY WORDS

INDIVIDUALISM:
the idea that we are fundamentally separate individuals

HUMANISM:
the ethical idea that we should see ourselves as individuals who are free to choose our own destinies

CLIMATE OF REASON

★ **With the European economic expansion into the "new world"** of the Americas and the scientific discovery that the Earth was not the center of a divinely ordered cosmos, but was one world among many others in a cosmological **system**, the simple certainties of Aristotelianism increasingly seemed like flimsy religious dogma. In this climate of intellectual transformation, new groups began to

Christopher Columbus sailed off and discovered the Americas

position themselves against the sources of ecclesiastical power. These groups held very different sets of values and espoused very different philosophies from those underlying Roman Catholicism.

THE POWER OF INDIVIDUALISM

* For early Humanists, the universe was not ordered by fate or divine agency, but was increasingly seen as having the potential to be shaped by the individual human will. This was the age of the self-made **Renaissance man**, and Renaissance culture would help support the rising tide of **individualism**. There was also a new spirit of economic entrepreneurialism from an increasingly geographically adventurous merchant class. In an age that idolized the strong-willed, the world-renouncing Catholic Church found itself increasingly out of touch with the popular mood.

INTELLECTUALS UNITE

* The intellectual opposition to the medieval world view began in the fifteenth century, during the **Renaissance**, with the Humanist ideas of **Desiderius Erasmus** (1466–1536), **Niccolò Machiavelli** (1469–1527), and **Michel de Montaigne** (1533–92). Each of these thinkers accepted Protagoras' (see page 57) idea that our own human world is the only world in existence, and that **we can make of this world what we will**.

we have proved through careful observation that all the planets move around the sun

Galileo

COPERNICUS AND GALILEO

Astronomers had proved, through a careful observation and measurement of the movement of the planets, that all the planets, even Earth, moved in varying orbits around the Sun. This was to shatter the Earth-centered cosmology that had underpinned the authority of the Roman Catholic Church, and not even Galileo's recanting of his discoveries under torture could alter the plain fact that the old cosmology's time was up.

Martin Luther and those articles

SPIRITUAL TRANSITION

* The transition away from a spiritual to a "modern" technocracy was, however, to take some 500 years to complete, and it was only with the French Revolution in 1789 that the so-called "quarrel between the ancients and the moderns" was to be resolved in a bloody victory for the moderns. This led to the rise of the modern state and the establishment of technocratic power in western Europe.

REFORMATION

At the start of the sixteenth century the growing problems facing the Catholic Church were further compounded by **Martin Luther** (1483–1546), who was about to begin his personal crusade to reform Christianity. Luther added to this new sense of individualism when he claimed that Christian belief was a matter of **personal faith** rather than objective truth.

THE MODERN STATE

* However, the new secular order did not emerge in any straightforward or simple way. It is beyond the scope of this story to offer any detailed account of how the new forms of nonreligious authority were constructed out of the remnants of decaying ecclesiastical political structures.

* The received view is that the break that occurred between the ancient and modern views of the universe involved a profound shift in both the structure and philosophical orientation of modern western societies.

WAYS OF CONTROL

* **However, it might be suggested that there are many more continuities between the medieval and modern worlds than is usually claimed**. They are both SYSTEMS OF SOCIAL AND POLITICAL CONTROL WHOSE POWER IS BASED ON THE ABILITY OF AN ELITE TO CONTROL, disseminate, and manipulate ideas.

* Sociologically speaking, both these worlds are divided into a PRIESTLY CLASS that controls these ideas and the rest of the universe that the priestly class attempts to control. The main difference in a modern technocracy is that it is not only people who are the objects of technocratic control. In modern societies, **nature** itself is increasingly subjected to the same kind of **controlling techniques** that were once applied to deviants and heretics.

the priestly class aspired to control the birds and the bees

* This use of thought to manipulate and control the natural world became instituted in the modern practice of **science**. Thus science slowly replaced religion as the most significant source of authoritative ideas in the modern world.

THE NEW MAGIC

In its attempts to control and organize nature, science could be seen as being somewhat like **magic**, and, in its attempts to provide a true account of the nature and workings of the cosmos, as being something like **religion**. Science can thus be viewed as a type of magic that is worshiped in its own right for the power that it is seen to exert on the world around us.

I'm the boss—go and build your nest now!

A MATHEMATICAL CLARITY

* So the new secular order of modern technocracy was to be built upon two "philosophical" foundations, Humanism and scientific rationalism. The latter "philosophy" viewed both nature and human societies as rationally ordered systems whose nature and workings could be understood by those practiced in the art of rational thought.

calculation has all the answers

Hobbes

ARITHMETIC

For the technocrats, as for Plato, the best account of rational thinking, or "rationality," is given by the traditional proofs of **geometry and arithmetic,** since these offered a model of procedural thinking that was seen to guarantee **truth.**

HOBBES THE EARLY RATIONALIST

* For the early rationalists, there was no more certain knowledge than mathematical knowledge, and so mathematics was seen by a generation of technocratic thinkers as the most clear, concise, and secure basis upon which to build the new technocratic edifice.

* **The first example of a "philosopher" who best exemplified this shift** in thinking was the Englishman **Thomas Hobbes** (1588–1679). Hobbes was writing during one of the most intense periods of disagreement between the ancients and the moderns, the English Civil wars (1642–48).

THE MONSTROUS CONTROLLER

★ According to Hobbes, people, if left to act according to their true natures, have no morals at all, and **altruism**—the idea that we should value each other nearly as much as we value ourselves—is an illusion. Hence human societies that lack adequate strong centers of power to control our inherent selfishness inevitably turn into evil anarchies where human life is "solitary, poor, nasty, brutish, and short." The only way to stem our natural dispositions, thought Hobbes, was to submit our will to an all-powerful **leviathan**—a kind of imaginary despot that by force or fear makes us live "civilized" lives.

mine, all mine (I'm essentially selfish)

THE READY RECKONER

★ Hobbes also thought that thinking had nothing to do with wondering, reflecting, or speculating as the early philosophers had claimed. He suggested that thinking was more like **calculating**, and so rationality was merely a cynical weighing-up of the pros and the cons. This was to become the psychological basis of modern economic theory, and Hobbes is very often viewed as laying the foundations for a future science of politics and society.

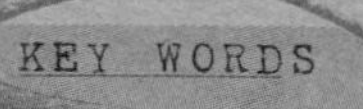

EGOISM:
the ethical idea that people ought to act according to their own self-interest

ALTRUISM:
the ethical idea that we ought to take others' interests into account when deciding what to do, even if this means denying our own desires and aspirations

LEVIATHAN:
powerful political authority devised to protect egoists from the antisocial consequences of their own nasty selfishness

Horrible humans

According to Hobbes, all humans are essentially selfish and motivated to improve their own lot, even if this means doing horrible things to other people. This is a philosophy that is sometimes known as egoism, and it underpins most technocratic ways of thinking, even the more contemporary varieties.

DESCARTES' RATIONALISM

★ Hobbes' French contemporary, Descartes (see pages 104-107), founded the school of modern rationalism. This school wanted to base all knowledge on abstract universal principles that were somehow innately in everybody. His most famous works are *The Discourse on Method* (1637) and *The Meditations* (1641), in which he tries to spell out the best and most reliable way to secure the truth in an age of conflicting opinions.

the solitary ego trapped by our own freedom

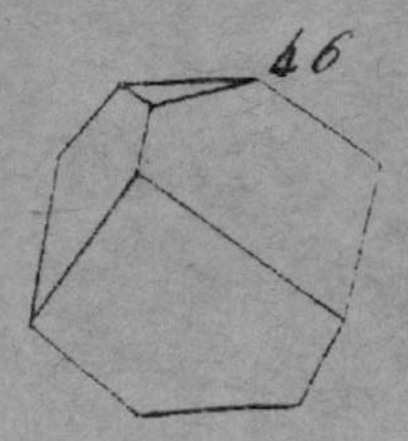

Coordinates

Because matter was defined essentially by its shape, the natural world, according to Descartes, could be entirely known by the application of **geometric principles**. To this end, Descartes devised **Cartesian geometry**, a coordinate system that could give an accurate mathematical representation of an object by mapping its extension in space.

A SIGNIFICANT CONTRIBUTION

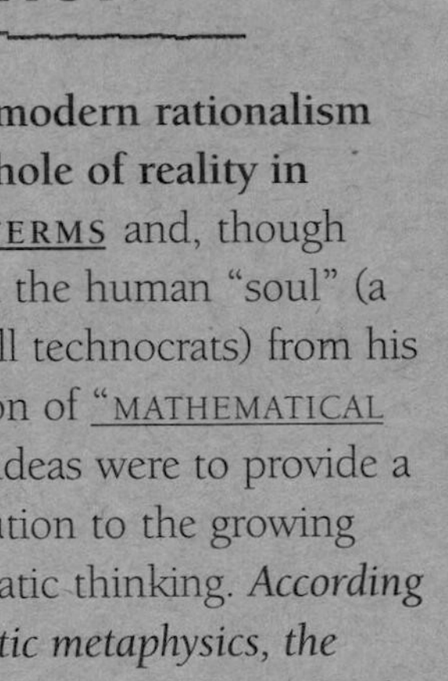

★ **The school of modern rationalism understood the whole of reality in** MATHEMATICAL TERMS and, though Descartes excluded the human "soul" (a term despised by all technocrats) from his metaphysical version of "MATHEMATICAL IMPERIALISM," his ideas were to provide a significant contribution to the growing corpus of technocratic thinking. *According to Descartes' dualistic metaphysics, the universe is comprised of two different kinds of basic stuff: mind and matter.* Mind was seen as an "EXTENSIONLESS THINKING SUBSTANCE" (**res cogitans**) and matter was understood as simply "EXTENSION IN TIME AND SPACE" (**res extensa**).

BEYOND DESCARTES

* Another feature of Descartes' thought was its manifest individualism. The ultimate source of epistemological authority for Descartes was Descartes himself. Knowledge was derived from the rational thinking of the **solitary ego**, a self that was viewed as being ENTIRELY SEPARATE FROM ITS NATURAL AND SOCIAL SURROUNDINGS.

you're such an individual

* Subsequent rationalists, for example **Benedict de Spinoza** (1632–77) and **Gottfried Leibniz** (1646–1716), developed Descartes' ideas still further and tried to place them on more secure metaphysical ground. They rejected Descartes' **dualism** on the grounds of incoherence and attempted to find a way of combining his rationalism with a metaphysical **monism**. Spinoza, a heretical Jew whose family fled Spain during the Inquisition, was a **materialist** who believed that the universe was made of matter governed by objective and knowable mathematical laws.

Leibniz

Leibniz believed that the universe consisted fundamentally of self-subsistent, individual **monads** who were governed by a rational consciousness that he understood to be rather like "calculation." So, according to Leibniz, everyone in the modern world is basically alone with their freedom to behave like a double-entry bookkeeper.

KEY WORDS

DUALISM: the metaphysical idea that the world is in reality two kinds of thing, usually mind and matter

RES COGITANS: Descartes' idea that we are essentially disembodied thinking beings

RES EXTENSA: Descartes' idea that material things are simply extended geometric shapes

RENÉ DESCARTES

* Descartes was born in France in 1596. As a youth he had been a devout Catholic, and his mature philosophy retained certain Catholic themes. He was educated by Jesuits and as young man was very impressed with the certainty and precision of mathematics. Rather surprisingly, he fought on the side of the Protestants against the Catholics in the Thirty Years War (1618-48) and it should therefore be of no surprise that ethical questions were not his main philosophical concern.

René Descartes and his imaginary demon

THE SKEPTICS

Descartes lived during a time when the authority of the Roman Catholic church was ebbing, and accepted notions of religious truth were being questioned. And as the old big truths crumbled, so the philistines started to reappear. The most extreme kind of philistine at this time were the **skeptics**. They claimed that there is no such thing as knowledge and that there is no difference between knowledge and illusion.

A METAPHYSICAL MAN

* **Descartes**' philosophy was basically an attempt to silence the **skeptics** who scoffed at the idea that we could know anything. To do this he had to find an example of a belief that was so **obviously true** that you would have to be nuts to deny it.

* Descartes set about this task with the diligent and methodical approach that had produced certain truths for him the past—he would find a method to get his example of CERTAIN

would I tell you a lie?

KNOWLEDGE. He used his **method of doubt** to do this.

* He would consider as false anything that was CAPABLE OF BEING DOUBTED and would expose all his beliefs to the most withering doubt imaginable. Any belief that survived this test would clearly be a good example of certain knowledge.

Descartes was skeptical of anything capable of being doubted

KEY WORDS

MALIGNANT DEMON: hypothetical doubt-inducing evil phantom
CERTAINTY: the only cure for the demon's poisonous doubt
COGITO: Descartes' most certain fact, the fact that he is thinking

BANISHING DEMONS

* To this end he invented a **malignant demon**. *Imagine, Descartes said, that your mind is controlled by an evil demon that makes all your beliefs, no matter how cherished, completely false. How do you know that all your beliefs are not the result of the evil designs of the deceiving demon?* Descartes thought that he did possess one true idea that even the evil demon could not make false: the idea that **he thought—for a thought that deceives is still a thought!** No one can doubt that they think, because to doubt that you think is still to think … EUREKA! The skeptic had been silenced and Descartes had found his example of certain knowledge. This is encapsulated in his famous maxim *cogito ergo sum*, **"I think therefore I am."**

dances with demons—who will win out?

...no, I heard mathematics is the latest thing

KEY WORDS

RATIONALISM:
the idea that the rational application of reason is our best guide to truth and knowledge

DUALISM:
the metaphysical idea that the world is in reality two kinds of thing, usually mind and matter

mathematics answers nature's mysteries

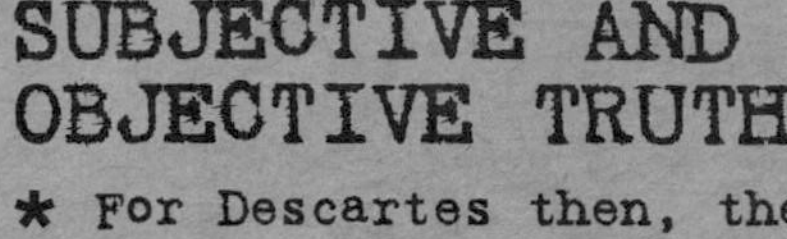

SUBJECTIVE AND OBJECTIVE TRUTH

★ For Descartes then, the start of all knowledge was the individual self, because this was the only thing on which anyone could rely as a source of knowledge in a rapidly changing world. However, we can see that Descartes' account of certain knowledge was still only subjective. He could not be sure of any objective truth without his belief in the existence of God as an epistemological guarantor.

A TECHNOCRAT AT HEART

★ Descartes' philosophy represented the most significant attempt in history to provide a philosophical foundation for technocratic ways of thinking. Descartes' dualistic metaphysics, which sees the universe as consisting of two fundamentally different kinds of stuff, the **mental** and the **material**, is sometimes known as **Cartesian dualism**. This split between thought and everything else is mirrored in the technocrat's belief that the world is divided into thinking experts and the unthinking masses.

Descartes tutoring the queen of Sweden

THE RATIONALISTS RULE

* Descartes tried to legitimize the technocratic idea that NATURE COULD BE UNDERSTOOD MATHEMATICALLY AND THAT IT WAS POSSIBLE TO PROVIDE A COMPLETE AND ACCURATE DESCRIPTION OF THE ENTIRE UNIVERSE USING NUMBERS ALONE. Technocrats liked this because it seemed to suggest that understanding the world was simply a matter of having the correct **mathematical information**.

* This means that KNOWLEDGE IS ONLY FOR THOSE WHO CAN APPRECIATE THE SUBTLE BEAUTY OF MATHEMATICAL KNOWLEDGE, and for Descartes, only those people who possessed the clarity of a rational mind could ever hope to see the truth. **The Church is dead!** Viva technocracy!

an illuminating moment

DESCARTES' ILLUMINATING MOMENT

Descartes lived in Holland from 1620, and it is there that his interest in philosophy began. He was said to have experienced a revelation of the fundamental truths of the universe. He wrote works on philosophy, optics, geometry, and on the nature of the soul. He left Holland for Stockholm in 1649 at the invitation of Queen Christina, where he died of pneumonia in 1650.

achoo

Descartes in his death throes

NEW FORMS OF CONTROL

* The rationalists developed ways of thinking about ourselves and the natural world that legitimized the new emerging systems of social and political control. Their attempts to understand both inner and outer nature in such overtly mathematical and mechanical ways provided them with epistemologically secure sources of information, honest data that would allow them to bring their own selves and the wider world under new and more "penetrating" forms of control.

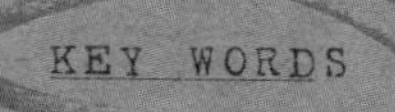

EMPIRICISM: the epistemological idea that all knowledge ultimately derives from the senses

A PRIORI PRINCIPLES: knowledge derived from reflective "armchair" thinking (such as "nothing can be red and green all over")

A POSTERIORI KNOWLEDGE: knowledge derived from observation

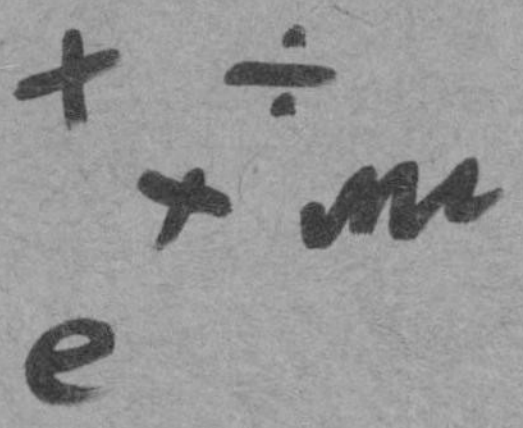

Bureaucracy

Rationalist ideas paved the way for the emergence of modern bureaucracy with its incessant coding and categorizing of human life. Some would say this converted Western culture into a harsh "kingdom of numbers," where power increasingly resided with the few who possessed the requisite powers of mathematical abstraction.

THE EMPIRICISTS

* In seventeenth-century England, there emerged a rival to rationalism—**empiricism**. According to this philosophy, the rationalists were wrong to claim that knowledge was grounded in the **a priori** (meaning "prior to experience") certainties of mathematics. On the contrary, for them, the only true and uncorrupted source of knowledge was **sense-experience,** and so all knowledge was **a posteriori** (meaning "after experience").

Isaac Newton

THE POWER OF SCIENCE

* The empiricists thought that we could only ever know something if we could acquaint ourselves with that thing through the senses, and they gave special attention to the epistemological powers inherent in human vision. This rather more "biblical" type of epistemology was modeled on (what was seen at the time to be) the successful practice of science.
* The "successes" of the new sciences of physics and chemistry that had been achieved by the extraordinary theorizings of **Robert Boyle** (1627–91) and **Isaac Newton** (1642–1727) were viewed by a new generation of admiring philosophers to be the result of a powerful epistemology that was the true source of the power of science.

Robert Boyle

Dangerous experiments

As we know, unprincipled experimentation can have unpleasant consequences for those objects experimented on. The scientific attempt to manipulate nature to reveal its deepest truths can lead, in certain instances, to some ugly ecological consequences.

AN AGE OF EXPERIMENT

* The empiricists believed that the new scientific knowledge had been the result of the scientists' careful **observation** and **measurement** of phenomena and their willingness to experiment with these phenomena to ascertain the precise, mathematical relationships that might exist between them. For the empiricists, it was experiment, not mathematical **proof**, that guaranteed knowledge, and their new "try it, you'll like it" epistemologies were to be a useful antidote to the mathematical excesses of its rival.

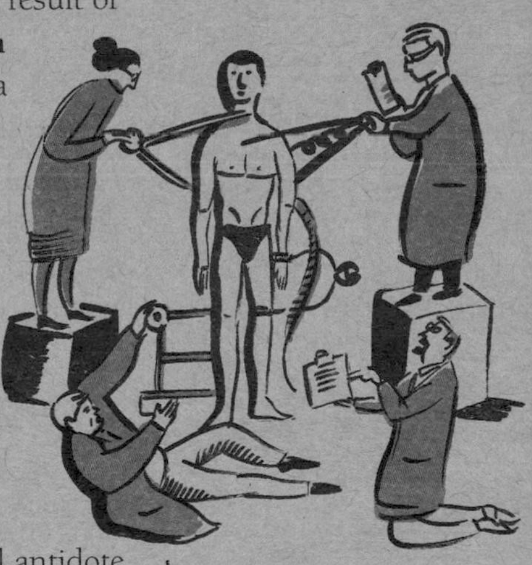

it's all a matter of measurement

THE KEY TO LOCKE

* The first empiricist philosopher of note was John Locke (1632-1704). Locke was an admirer of the ideas of the chemist Robert Boyle and was an influential anti-Catholic involved in Protestant politics. He wrote extensively on a wide range of philosophical issues, and he became philosophically famous both as an epistemologist and as a political philosopher.

a ripe tomato

IDEAS

For Locke all ideas were basically of two kinds, **simple ideas** and **complex ideas.** The former were viewed as being something like simple unanalyzable experiences—like, for example, the tang of a ripe tomato. Complex ideas, like, for example "horse," were seen as being constructed out of such simple sense-perceptions.

INNOCENCE AND EXPERIMENT

* Locke was also famous for his empiricist epistemology and disagreed with the rationalists in that he claimed that individuals were born with no innate knowledge at all. He viewed the mind of the newborn baby as being rather like a blank slate (**tabula rasa**) on which experience was to write its knowledgeable story.

no innate knowledge, but crabby all the same

* In addition, Locke's philosophy attempted to retain something of the metaphysics of the Continental rationalists. He believed, like Aristotle, that the most basic metaphysical category is SUBSTANCE, which he viewed as being the basic "STUFF" upon which all the observable empirical properties of a thing were somehow "supported."

John Locke

PHILOSOPHY'S NEW ROLE

philosophy the laborer?

* Locke thought that philosophy should be about deciding between objects that are suitable for scientific investigation and objects that are not. He thus defined the role of philosophy as being the "**under-laborer to the sciences**" revealing himself as very much a technocrat at heart.

* Locke's SCHOLASTIC NOTION of substance was criticized severely by subsequent empiricists such as **George Berkeley**. Berkeley was born in Ireland in 1658 and became an Anglican bishop. He criticized Locke's **scientific realism**, that is, his idea that the true reality of the cosmos was given to us by the new physics.

Two kinds of properties

Locke suggested that all the properties residing in things were of two kinds: **primary qualities** (like size, shape, material composition) and **secondary qualities** (like color, smell, beauty). The former were seen as the objective properties inherent in a thing, and hence the true source of scientific knowledge about that thing. The latter were seen as mere **subjective appearances** and hence should be of no concern to an objectively oriented science.

KEY WORDS

PRIMARY QUALITIES: the properties that objects possess in themselves (like shape)

SECONDARY QUALITIES: the properties that objects possess only because there is an individual person perceiving them (like redness)

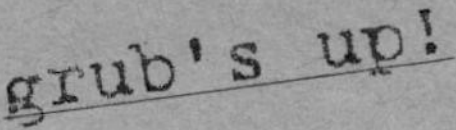

the way to a man's heart is through his stomach

THE ROUTE TO PHILISTINISM

★ Locke's philosophy had claimed that reality was simply made up of material bodies possessing just those primary qualities presupposed by their mode of mechanical functioning. This was anathema to Berkeley. He thought that such a philosophy, in denying the reality of our subjective inner lives, would lead us into the philistine world of philosophical skepticism. And indeed this is what David Hume (see pages 114-17) was later to argue.

How can we know?

Berkeley asked in his *Treatise Concerning the Principles of Human Knowledge* (1710), how Locke could ever be justified in claiming that his external world actually exists. If "red" and "blue" are merely subjective constructs, then why not also the so-called primary qualities of "shape" and "size?"

SKEPTICISM

★ Skepticism is the idea that we cannot have any knowledge of the external world and that we should give up the search for truth as an illusion. Locke's philosophy, by opening up a gap between the subjective and objective features of reality, leaves an epistemological gap where the skeptics can find space for their "evil" doings.

INSTRUMENTALISM

Berkeley's philosophy has been influential in those branches of technocratic thought that claim that scientific theories aren't really true descriptions of the world, but merely useful tools for predicting and controlling events—an epistemological position that is sometimes known as **instrumentalism.**

SEEING IS BELIEVING

★ For Berkeley, **reality was essentially subjective**, and for this reason his philosophy is sometimes called **subjective idealism** (idealism is the metaphysics that claims that reality is all in the mind). He argued that **esse est**

reality is all in the mind

percipi (to be is to be perceived) and avoided the charge of **solipsism** (or the idea that everything only exists in **one's own mind**) by claiming that everything existed, objectively, in the mind of God.

A PASSIONATE MAN

* David Hume was to develop Berkeley's ideas further. He accepted that **empiricism**, if taken seriously, leads to **skepticism**. However, Hume thought that this wasn't much for us to be concerned about, because no matter what the philosophers might say, we will all still carry on believing what we do anyway. Reason and reflection, for Hume, were not paths to truth but the **slaves of the passions**. And the passions of human life—the desire for food, for games, and for good company—were what life should be all about. Hume can thus be seen as a "philosopher of common sense."
* So, to some extent, if we accept his conclusions, we must concede that empiricism, even though it claims to speak for technocratic science, is maybe more closely related to philistinism than to technocratic ways of thinking.

KEY WORDS

IDEALISM: the metaphysical idea that the cosmos, as we humans understand it, is the creation of at least one human mind

SOLIPSISM: the idea that the entire cosmos is the creation of my mind

INSTRUMENTALISM: the idea that scientific theories are not true, but are "useful fictions"

DAVID HUME

★ Hume's most famous work, *A Treatise of Human Nature* (1739-40), was dedicated to extending the experimental methods of the empirical sciences to the understanding of the human mind.

poking around in the brain

HUME'S MIND GAMES

★ Hume was tired of the "endless disputes" of the classical philosophers, and he sought the truth via the more direct route of empirical observation. Hume was thus an arch-empiricist who believed the human sense-experience was the source of all true knowledge and that any knowledge claim not ultimately based on this was nothing more than "sophistry and illusion."

everything is in our own minds

SCOTTISH ENLIGHTENMENT

David Hume was born in Scotland in 1711. He was brought up in a strict Presbyterian family, and the austere world of Scottish Protestantism was to instil in him a profound distaste for the excesses of metaphysical speculation. He was one of the key figures, alongside the famous economist Adam Smith, in the so-called **Scottish Enlightenment.**

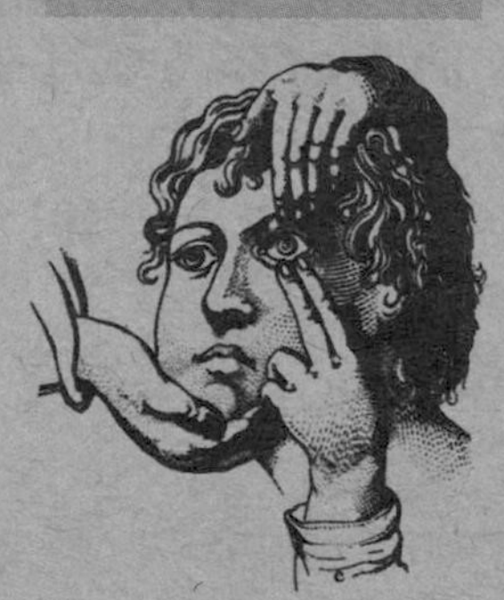

senses and sensibility

The significance of his thought lies in the fact that he was the first philosopher to offer a thorough account of the difficulties inherent in all empiricist philosophies.

Hume used careful observation to reach his conclusions

THE NATURE OF THE MIND

* Hume's empiricism came from his belief that it is only by CAREFUL OBSERVATION OF PHENOMENA that we can ever hope to develop knowledge of the world external to the human mind as well as the internal world of personal psychological experience.
* **In his quest to discover the laws that governed the workings of the human mind, Hume relied on information derived from his own internal self-observation** or **self-introspection**. From closely inspecting the nature and workings of his own thoughts, he believed that he had DISCOVERED THE TRUE NATURE OF THE HUMAN MIND—that it was made up of **impressions** derived from the senses and **ideas** that were "generalized" from these impressions.

Newton of the mind

Hume, like many of his contemporaries, had been very impressed with Isaac Newton's new physics. Hume was particularly impressed by the absence of religion and metaphysics in Newton's cosmology. He tried to apply Newton's mechanical principles to understanding the nature and workings of the human mind. His ambition was to be the "Newton of the mind" and hoped that his philosophy would help to demystify the human world in the way that Newton's physics had the natural world. Hume was, then, to all intents and purposes, an early **psychologist,** and he attempted to establish a foundational philosophy for a new a "science of the mind." The fact that he tried to reduce the workings of the human mind to a simple mechanism means that Hume's philosophy is the intellectual grandparent of those psychological theories that view the human mind as a computer and a human being as a "meat robot."

beware: all impressions come from association

IMPRESSION AND ASSOCIATION

* According to Hume, impressions are converted into ideas by a process of association. For example, we construct a general idea of a swan out of the myriad impressions that have been associated with particular, swans that we may have seen.

Hume

A party animal

Hume's atheism was not merely an Enlightenment fad; he lived it. Hume was a real party animal and remained so until he died of cancer in 1776. The fact that he lived his philosophy and stayed cheerful to the end made Hume's life, like Socrates' before him, a truly **philosophical life**.

WHAT COLOR IS A SWAN?

* For most people in the northern hemisphere, THE GENERAL IDEA OF A SWAN IS OF A WHITE, LONG-NECKED BIRD OFTEN SEEN FLOATING ON THE SURFACE OF LAKES.

* This idea, according to **Hume**, is a product of a chain of associations between the impressions that people in the northern hemisphere typically have of swans. However, people in some parts of the southern hemisphere, where many swans are black, will have

since when have swans been black?

different impressions of swans, and so will form a different idea of what all swans are like.

TRUTH AND THE PAST

★ **So, for Hume, general truths and ideas are formed by the associative powers of the mind** out of the material of raw experience. ALL KNOWLEDGE IS MADE BY US (a point that was later to be developed by Kant) AND ALL TRUTH IS CONTINGENT (upon the context that individuals find themselves in). There is no such thing as a necessary truth (a truth that must be true, no matter what), and even our most certain beliefs only appear so because the world has happened to behave in particular ways for us in the past. So Hume denied that knowledge, in the strict sense of grasping the "TRUE NATURE OF REALITY," was possible at all, showing that a consistent empiricist philosophy leads to **skepticism**.

A COMMITTED ATHEIST

★ Hume was also famous for his staunch atheism and, in his *Dialogues Concerning Natural Religion*, one of the most beautifully written works in the history of philosophy, he pilloried all the scholastic attempts to provide proof of God's existence. He showed that all the proof **begged the question** of God's existence, as they assumed his existence prior to their conclusions.

You can't rely on the past

Even though we believe with almost 100 percent certainty that all swans are white, that it always rains in Seattle, or that there will never be a completely free and just society anywhere in the modern world, we can, according to Hume, never **know** this to be true. This is because we can never **prove** that the future will be like the past without relying on *a priori* reasoning, which the empirically-minded Hume rejected.

why does it always rain in Seattle?

THE UTILITARIANS

* By the beginning of the nineteenth century, technocratic thought was at the height of its powers. This can be seen in the writings of the English utilitarians, who tried to base human morality not on the altruistic emotions of sympathy and concern for others, but on a simple rational calculus.

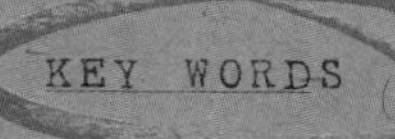

KEY WORDS

UTILITARIAN: an unprincipled person who generally believes that the "ends justify the means"

ROMANTIC: a person who believes in the creative powers of the self

Bentham thought criminals could be reformed

THE GREATEST HAPPINESS OF THE GREATEST NUMBER

* According to utilitarians such as Jeremy Bentham (1748–1832), an action was good if it produced the greatest happiness in the greatest number of people affected by it.

* Crude versions of utilitarian ethics would say that if you kill a small child to save a city, this is not just prudent, but an entirely moral way of behaving. The utilitarians would impose a rigid system with no regard for emotion or compassion. Thus the extreme forms of this technocratic way of thinking suffer from the same moral limitations as ancient paganism.

THE ANTITECHNOCRATIC BACKLASH

However, the end of the eighteenth century saw the emergence of new antisystemic, antitechnocratic movements throughout Europe. These movements complained that technocratic ways of thinking had led to an **atomization and dehumanization of human societies**.

the Romantics brought art back into philosophy

* They argued that there was no mention of culture and community in the individualistic writings of the technocratic "philosophers," and they tried to develop new ways of thinking that emphasized the importance of art, creativity, and spontaneity. They also longed for a sense of belonging in a world that they thought was being "drained of significance" by the cold abstractions of technocratic thought.

Jeremy Bentham

The panopticon

Bentham also had ideas about penal reform, and he is the originator the modern "liberal" view that we shouldn't punish criminals but try to change their behavior instead. To this end, he devised his own prison, the panopticon, a star-shaped building where the prison guard could see all the prisoners from his tower, but the prisoners were not aware that they were being watched. This regime was meant to leave prisoners alone with their guilt to contemplate their futures. Strangeways prison, in Manchester, England, is said to have been designed according to this principle and by all accounts it was, until recently, as barbaric a place as anyone could possibly imagine. So much the worse for Bentham's model!

CHAPTER 5

ROMANTICS AND REVOLUTIONARIES

*** Immanuel Kant (1724-1834) was possibly the most important philosopher to emerge from the eighteenth-century philosophical movement known as the Enlightenment. He was born in Königsberg in East Prussia (now the site of a Russian military base) in 1724, and he spent almost his whole life in the city.**

Kant manages to turn technocratic philosophy on its head

SCIENCE AND ETHICS

* As we shall see, **Kant** manages to TURN TECHNOCRATIC PHILOSOPHY ON ITS HEAD and is the first modern philosopher to offer a more **truly hopeful** philosophy, a way of looking at the world that places the autonomous, creative human person at its center.

* **In the eighteenth century, many philosophers came to the conclusion** that the rational methods of science were not only the most secure ways of getting to the truth, as rationalists and the empiricists had thought, but were also, in some sense, **ethical principles**.

the autonomous, creative human person at the world's center

human history is the struggle to build a rational culture

BUILDING THE FUTURE

★ According to the ENLIGHTENMENT PHILOSOPHERS, like the French philosopher **Voltaire** (1694–1778), human history is the struggle to build a rational culture that does away with all mystery and superstition and tries to build a future society on principles revealed by the divine light of rational (including scientific) knowledge.

Voltaire

rational knowledge provides the building blocks for future society

A BRAVE NEW SCIENTIFIC WORLD

★ So, according to this new wave of **technocratic sympathizers**, the new knowledge of both ourselves and the natural world that had been given to us by the hard-earned results of scientific inquiry would empower state planners and other technocratic strategists in their attempt to build a rational future.

WORTH THE EFFORT

Kant's writing, especially the famous *Critique of Pure Reason* (1781), is difficult and is full of the most subtle conceptual distinctions imaginable. But for those willing to persist through what seems at times an intellectual thicket of almost impenetrable obscurity, the philosophical rewards are great.

scientific knowledge should be used to build a new, perfect society

THE GOOD SOCIETY

★ Many Enlightenment thinkers agreed with the Renaissance philosopher Francis Bacon (1562-1626), who claimed that scientific knowledge should be used to build a "new Atlantis," a society where knowledge is used to perfect the ills of society.

reflecting on rational thought

REASON RULES OK?

★ They thought that if reason and rationality were allowed to become the organizing principles of modern societies, this would inevitably lead to the development of a truly **"good society,"** a society built upon the values of social progress, tolerance, and an obedience to the **"general will"** of all.

a society where knowledge is used to remedy social ills

ENLIGHTENMENT

This was also a period in European cultural history when many philosophers believed that rational reflection would allow us to truly know ourselves and so let human beings to become "transparent to themselves" in the pure reflecting "mirror of reason."

* With the Enlightenment then, we can see how the ideas found in the works of technocratic philosophers were increasingly used to *justify the new utopian ideas* of the technocrats and how philosophy increasingly came to view itself as A TOOL OF SOCIAL ENGINEERING.

THE LIMITS OF REASON

* Kant, like Hume before him, thought that philosophical reflection would bring to the surface the hidden workings of the human mind. However, Kant, like Hume, was skeptical about the powers that some rationalist philosophers had attributed to reason and rationality, and he wanted to show that REASON HAD ITS LIMITS.

Kant's philosophy reflects upon itself

KANT'S SOLUTION

* To this end, Kant turned the mirror of philosophical reflection on the principles of rational thought themselves. Kant refused to get carried away by the utopian possibilities of science. He tried not only to demonstrate that science was built upon rational principles, but also that **these rational principles were only sources of knowledge when applied correctly**.

Self-knowledge

Kant's philosophical reflections are unusual in that they include themselves as objects in their own reflections. To this extent, Kant's thought, like that of Heraclitus (see pages 38–39) resembles the self-referring sketches of Escher.

A FALSE PHILOSOPHY

* Kant had been impressed by Hume's skeptical empiricism, but rather than accept Hume's conclusion, Kant argued that all Hume had really shown was that empiricism is false. He argued thus: "A consistent empiricism denies that we can know anything at all. We do know things. Therefore empiricism is a false philosophy."

we are the mocking skeptics

KEY WORDS

TRANSCENDENTAL REASONING: "backwards reasoning" from a fact to what must exist for that fact to be true (like any object must exist in 3-D space)

SYNTHETIC *A PRIORI* PRINCIPLES: active "organizing" principles of the human mind (like space has three dimensions)

BACK TO KNOWLEDGE

* How, then, according to Kant, do we know? **He argued that empiricists** had been led into the DARK WATERS OF THE PHILISTINES because empiricists viewed the human mind as a **passive mechanism** that could only construct certain **habits of mind** out of SIMPLE SENSORY INPUTS.

* However, we **do** know things. Hence, for Kant, philosophy must start from what we do know and then "argue backward" to show how it is possible for us to know such things.

* This ARGUING BACKWARD to reveal **the conditions of possibility** of all human thought and action was called **transcendental reasoning** by Kant.

THE ACTIVE MIND

* By using this type of reasoning, Kant claimed that human knowledge was **produced** (not found or discovered) by the human mind's ability to **synthesize** sensory input into significant meaning.

* This could only be done because the human mind provided the basic concepts of space, time, number, identity, etc., that were responsible for organizing our sense experiences (or, as Kant called them, **intuitions**) into meaningful thoughts.

* The empiricists, according to Kant, had neglected this **active input** from the human mind, and so, according to him, it was not surprising that they had difficulty avoiding the jibes of the mocking skeptic.

MIND SYNTHESIS

* Kant called these synthesizing principles of the human mind **synthetic** *a priori* principles. They included the mathematical truths of the rationalists and moral truths as well. For Kant, statements like, "KILLING PEOPLE FOR FUN IS OK BY ME!" were, like the statement, "Two plus two equals ninety-six," *a priori* false, and so Kant can be seen as **extending philosophical rationalism** into the realm of moral and political philosophy.

killing people for fun is OK by me!

Possible knowledge

For Kant, "intuitions without concepts are blind." Thus, though the empiricists were correct to rail against the excesses of rationalist *a priori* philosophizings, they needed his philosophical spectacles to see that knowledge was possible after all.

intuitions without concepts are blind

Kant's mission

Kant's desire was to discover the principles of the physical universe and the "moral universe within." His philosophy thus tries to combine scientific rationalism and the romantic concern for "the self."

out damn spot!
out I say

THE WORLD OF APPEARANCES

* However, there was much more to Kant's thinking than this. Because he claimed that all our meaningful experience of the world, including all meaningful experience of ourselves, was created by the human mind, then the human mind was not part of nature, but was somehow outside it—a philosophical position that has become known as transcendental idealism.

human brain

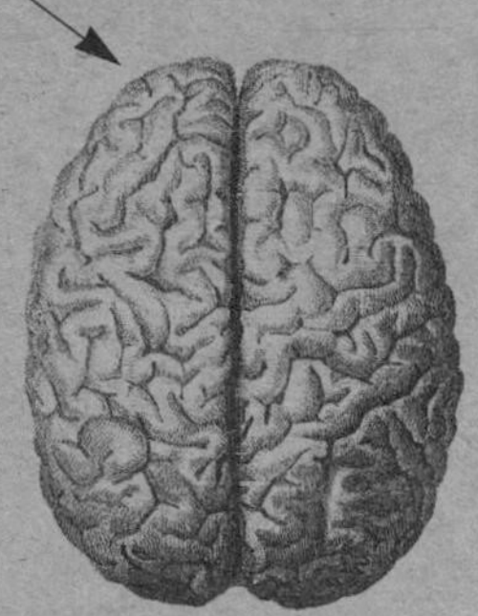

on the outside, looking in

KANT'S INFLUENCE

What Kant's philosophy really managed to achieve was to reignite the philosophical passions of artists and dreamers. Hurrah for Kant!

THE CREATIVE SELF

* For **Kant**, the only world that we know is the PHENOMENAL WORLD OF APPEARANCES, and we can never know what things in themselves ("*Ding an sich*") are really like. But his rational philosophical reflections showed him that there must also exist a **synthesizing subject**, which is the *individual creative self* who creates his own world through the powers of AUTONOMOUS RATIONAL JUDGEMENT.

we all create our own world

* For Kant then, what lay in between **concepts** and **intuitions** was individual human judgement; the application of concepts to intuitions was more like AN ART THAN A RATIONAL PROCEDURE.

I sentence you to decide for yourself

calculation couldn't cover it

A ROMANTIC THINKER

* KANT'S PHILOSOPHY IS DIFFICULT, but a careful reading shows that he was much more of a **romantic thinker** than he was a rationalist. In his view, though all humans possessed **rational *a priori* principles**, their application was something of an art and not simply an act of mathematical calculation. Because of this, thinking was more like an autonomous use of the imagination than accounting, reckoning, or other forms of actuarial thinking.

KEY WORDS

TRANSCENDENTAL IDEALISM:
the metaphysical idea that the world is real at the level of appearances but a creation of the mind in reality

INTUITIONS:
raw sensory material that is only meaningful once it is conceptualized by the mind

JUDGEMENT:
the art of applying concepts to intuitions

now, where did I put that concept?

ROMANTICS AND AESTHETES

★ In the wake of Kant's philosophy came the romantics, who viewed both mind and nature as unified and saw art and aesthetic interpretation as the source of all true knowledge. For the romantics, such as Friedrich von Schelling (1775-1854) and the poet and historian Friedrich Schiller (1759-1805), the genuine bringer of knowledge was the artistic genius rather than the experimental scientist.

ARTISTIC VISION

The romantics opposed those philosophers who claimed that the methods of science and mathematics were the only route to true knowledge. For them, it was the creative activity of the artist, who created his/her world from nothing, that gave a truer picture of the nature of human understanding.

the romantic unity of mind and nature

KEY WORDS

GEIST: the universal spirit of which each individual mind is a part

DIALECTIC: the principle determining the movement of Geist through history

NEW SYNTHESIS

★ **By the beginning of the nineteenth century, various philosophers** made new attempts to try to COMBINE RATIONALISM AND ROMANTICISM into a new **"higher order"** philosophy. The most famous

artists 5, geeks 0

attempt to achieve this new synthesis between seemingly competing philosophies can be seen in the works of German **Georg Wilhelm Friedrich Hegel** (1770–1831).

Hegel requires serious homework

HEGEL AND HISTORY

★ Hegel accepted Kant's idealism and viewed reality as the product of the activity of a **rational mind**. However, this mind was a very different kind of thing from the solitary Cartesian ego of the rationalists (including Kant). For Hegel, MIND WAS A KIND OF **universal spirit** (*GEIST*) THAT MOVED THROUGH TIME AND SPACE. Reason was viewed as the underlying principle that governed the movement of this spirit through history (a very Heraclitean theme). Put crudely, the contradictions at the heart of Geist were the rational "engine" of historical change.

DIALECTICS

★ For Hegel, the movement of spirit through history was governed by a **dialectical process**. *By this he meant that the contradictions in the universal spirit could be understood as being like two sides of an argument* (thesis and antithesis) that were resolved as a synthesis of the two. This process, he thought, continued until all the contradictions of the spirit had resolved themselves. At this final point of history, Hegel thought that the spirit had attained complete knowledge of itself.

Hard work

Confused? Well, Hegel's philosophical writings present some of the most difficult philosophical concepts in the history of philosophy. The German philosopher **Herbert Marcuse** (1898–1979) claimed that, to do his ideas full justice, one should spend at least six hours reading each page of Hegel's most famous text, *The Phenomenology of Spirit* (1807).

STRENGTH AND WEAKNESS

* At its simplest, Hegel's philosophy states that history is a social process driven by contradictions between competing systems of ideas. This "contradiction" was viewed as being rather like the struggle between master and slave, a struggle that could only be resolved once the master finally recognized the slave as a free person. So ideas struggle for recognition: once the "weaker" ideas are recognized as valid and significant by the "stronger," a change occurs in the stronger dominant idea. At this point a new set of ideas emerges that supersedes both. Hegel called this a dialectical process, a process of historical change that produces new and better forms of knowledge via a process of thesis, antithesis, and, finally, a new synthesis.

is this the end of history?

THE END OF HISTORY

* When, according to Hegel, would history end? Well, clearly when there are no contradictions left between rival systems of ideas. He thought this happened in 1806 when Napoleon defeated the Prussian army at the battle of Jena. According to Hegel, this battle represented the final triumph of the ideas that had motivated the French Revolution: ideas of **liberty, equality, and fraternity**. This seems such a silly idea as to be almost unbelievable. But a contemporary

American philosopher, **Francis Fukuyama**, also claimed that history had ended, this time with the disbanding of the former Soviet Union. This failure of the main system of opposition to modern capitalism heralded, he said, the final triumph of the liberal idea of the inalienable rights of the solitary individual consumer.

spitting images—British leaders

we must do something to relieve the boredom

* We are now, according to him, living in a **"post-historical world"** where NOTHING MUCH HAPPENS AND THE MOST PRESSING SOCIAL PROBLEM IS BOREDOM. However, thankfully, most of us are still curious about the future course of history. Fukuyama, like many others, just got a bit philosophically carried away by the end of the cold war.

A political example

If you take British politics in the 1980s, we can see Margaret Thatcher's ideas as the dominant thesis and Neil Kinnock's ideas as the weaker antithesis. The final Hegelian synthesis of these two ideas is the ideas of Tony Blair's **New Labor Party**. Blair's ideas will eventually produce their own antithesis and so on until the **end of history.**

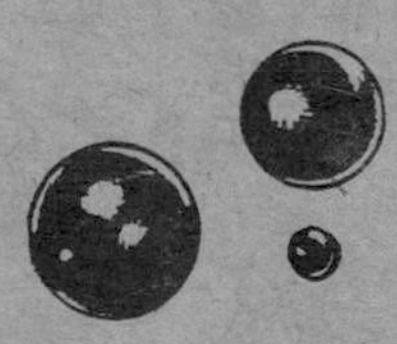

HEGEL'S LASTING INFLUENCE

★ Hegel was a rationalist philosopher in that he believed in reason and progress. Not surprisingly, he ended up being something of a technocrat when he argued that the highest form of human social organization was the nineteenth-century absolutist Prussian state.

KEY WORDS

MATERIALISM: the metaphysical idea that everything is made of matter
BOURGEOISIE: capital-owning social class
PROLETARIAT: labor-selling social class

which direction was philosophy going in?

HISTORY MAN

For Hegel it is our understanding of history, not science, that offers us the best way to understand ourselves and our environment. The fact that he wondered, "What is history?" and "In what direction is history moving?" makes Hegel a philosopher of supreme importance.

THE GOOD OF FLUX

★ However, there is much to commend in Hegel's philosophy. His was the first modern philosophy to accept the Heraclitean idea that flux and change are part of the very nature of existence.

★ Hegel also avoided the usual technocratic championing of science and argued that historical self-reflection was the way to ascertain the truth. However, he said that truths derived by this method were ephemeral and a product of historical circumstance.

a change is as good as a rest, you know

MARX'S MAKEOVER OF HEGEL

* **Hegel's ideas spawned a minor philosophical industry in their own right.** The most famous Hegelian was **Karl Marx** (1818–83) (see pages 134–37). Marx was very taken with Hegel's dialectical version of historical change, but he despised Hegel's idealism and thought that this part of his philosophy was NOTHING MORE THAN WOOLY MYSTICISM.

some periods of human history reveal horrifying insights

* Marx attempted to make Hegel's ideas more compatible with a **materialist metaphysics**. He argued that the true engine of progressive historical change was not a conflict between abstract systems of ideas, but was a REAL CONFLICT between social classes, groups that had **very different material interests**.

Lenin

The just society

Marx saw the most significant class conflict in the modern world as that between the bourgeoisie (bosses) and the proletariat (workers). This conflict would finally be resolved by a victory for the proletariat in a bloody social revolution, followed by the dictatorship of the proletariat and, finally, the withering away of all forms of social control and the emergence of truly free and just society of independent producers. However, in the hands of Vladimir Lenin (1870–1924), Marxism forgot about this historical happy ending.

Paris

HUMANS AS COMMODITIES

* Karl Marx was born in Trier, in what is now Germany, in 1818. In 1844, he moved to Paris, where he became acquainted with the radical politics of the new "working-class movement." His early philosophical work, *The Economic and Philosophical Manuscripts*, was profoundly humanist, concerned with how humans can develop through free creative activity.

AGAINST CAPITALISM

* Marx thought that the majority of Europe's laboring population were denied the opportunity to develop themselves fully as individuals because they were forced to sell their labor to exploitative capitalists: greedy businessmen who valued working people as sources of profit instead of human beings. Humans were thus reduced to abstract commodities that could be exchanged for any other commodity of similar price.

the human conveyor belt

★ **In this system, according to Marx, workers** were essentially **alienated** from their true selves. According to Marx, this meant that working people were estranged from their very being. Their time was not their own and the efforts of their labor, the products that they produced, were not for their own use, but for profitable sale on the open market. Marx was a **political philosopher** who sought to expose the injustices of modern capitalist societies. His idea of the "good society" was derived from his idea of the nature of premodern forms of social life where the dominant form of work was individual **craft production** for communal **use**, not economic **exchange**.

FOUNDING COMMUNISM

★ Marx left Paris and eventually returned to Germany, where he became heavily involved in working-class politics. He founded the **Communist League**, with his lifelong friend and colleague **Friedrich Engels** (1820–95), and in 1848 he wrote the *Communist Manifesto*, a pamphlet that was written more for the purposes of political agitation and propaganda than for philosophical reasons. In this work he claims that capitalism is really a kind of hell on earth, where "all that is sold melts into air" and "everything sacred is profaned." It is in this work that he introduces the philosophy of history for which he subsequently achieved fame.

Creative freedom

The fact that he was a passionate believer in human creativity and freedom and that he saw the craft production of the past in essentially idyllic terms is what makes the early Marx a **romantic philosopher.**

Marx

YOUNG HEGELIANS

Marx studied philosophy at the University of Berlin and was profoundly influenced by the materialist philosophy of the so-called **young Hegelian movement,** which attempted to use Hegel's essentially conservative philosophy as a tool of radical social criticism.

A revolutionary philosopher

Marx's whole approach to philosophy was captured by his famous *Eleventh Thesis on Feuerbach*, in which he claimed that "philosophers only describe the world, the point is to change it." It would seem then that Marx was not really a philosopher at all but a revolutionary committed to social and political change. Marx correctly foresaw that twentieth-century societies would be driven by a conflict between workers and their bosses. Hence he was, along with Nietzsche, one of the chief prophets of the modern age.

Marx

CLASS WAR

* According to Marx, all human history can be seen as a series of class struggles. The most significant class conflict of the medieval feudal world was between the merchant class and the old feudal aristocracy. The resolution of this conflict was a new social system, capitalism. But capitalism, though it pretended otherwise, was also class-ridden. The engine of modern history under capitalism, Marx believed, would be the political struggle between the bourgeoisie and the proletariat.

DEMISE OF CAPITALISM

* This struggle would lead to the eventual demise of capitalism and the emergence of a communist society where everybody lived according to the maxim **"from each according to their abilities, to each according to their needs."** The mature Marx moved away from his humanist and Hegelian roots and tried to construct a science of society. He thought that the most basic level of all human societies is the economic level of material production, and that people are, in the last analysis, driven by their material needs (for food, clothing, enjoyment).

AN ALTERNATIVE ECONOMICS

the reality for some

* Marx attempted to found his new science on an alternative economics to the one that had been invented by the classical economists **Adam Smith** (1723–90) and **David Ricardo** (1772–1823). These economists had claimed that modern capitalism was a free market of selfish "profit-maximizing" individuals and that free markets were the most rational way of allocating resources. Marx tried to expose Smith and Ricardo's theories as **ideologies**—that is, as **false accounts** of the nature of human social life that mask the brutal truth of life for the majority of people in modern capitalist societies.

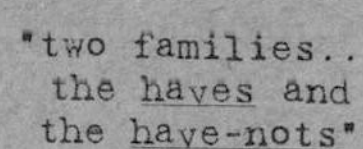

"two families... the haves and the have-nots"

* Marx put forward his alternative economic theory, the so-called **labor theory of value**, which claimed that the true value of a thing is not given by its price, but by the amount of **time** taken to produce it. He thus showed that the workers were the true source of all value in the world and that this has been unfairly appropriated by the capitalist class.

KEY WORDS

ALIENATION: state of psychological distress when people don't know who they really are

IDEOLOGIES: sets of ideas that create the illusion that the world is basically just and free, and so mask the harsh realities of modern capitalism

FREEDOM AT A PRICE

* In the middle of the nineteenth century there emerges a particularly depressing variety of romantic thought. With the ideas of the Danish philosopher Soren Kierkegaard (1813-55), we can see a new cultural pessimism about the nature and significance of human freedom. In his book *Either/Or*, Kierkegaard highlights the psychological costs of modern freedom. He points out that for most people life seems to present a series of choices that the individual has to resolve alone, without the help of reason or tradition or religious faith.

SCHOPENHAUER

Another notable depressive romantic philosopher was **Arthur Schopenhauer** (1788–1860). He, like Kierkegaard, was concerned with the psychological downside of being free. In his case, being free means the **liberation** of a will that can never be satisfied. Human life is therefore destined to be one of disappointment. Like a good romantic, Schopenhauer claimed that the true meaning of life lay in the consolations offered to its dispirited hosts by **art.**

PAINFUL EXISTENCE

* In *Sickness Unto Death*, Kierkegaard sees modern existence as being governed by some very painful emotional states: anxiety about choice, dread of the future, and futility in the face of death. His ideas were later to influence the dark and brooding writings of the twentieth-century existentialist novelist-philosophers: Franz Kafka, Jean-Paul Sartre, and Albert Camus.

Kierkegaard was very pessimistic about human freedom

★ **Schopenhauer's ideas were developed further by Friedrich Nietzsche** (see pages 140–43). Nietzsche saw the human world as being the expression of the **will to power** of "strong figures" who had the inner vitality to create their own meanings for themselves. For Nietzsche, THE POINT OF LIFE WAS NOT TO SIT AROUND GETTING DEPRESSED about the meaninglessness of modern technocracy, but to ESCAPE INTO A NEW WORLD OF YOUR OWN CREATION, a world where truly noble values and beautiful experiences govern your life.

THE ROMANTIC VISION

★ The romantics offered new philosophies that pointed to a new and different kind of society from the one constructed by the technocrats and their philosophical apologists. The romantics offered a vision of a society that was at once more EMOTIONAL AND NATURAL than its over-controlled and technological opponent.

Ugly romance

The politics that arose out of romantic thinking led to some of the most ugly moments in modern history. Marx's ideas were used to support the horrors of Stalinism, while Nietzsche's ideas influenced Nazi ideology. These romantic visions of society offer us no escape.

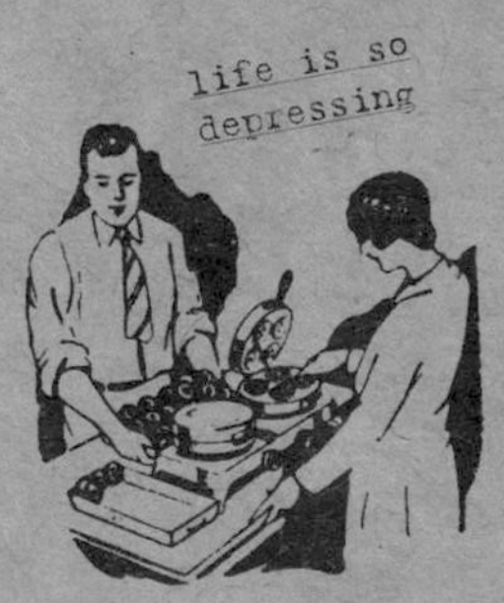

FRIEDRICH NIETZSCHE

Nietzsche

★ Friedrich Nietzsche was the first great philosopher after the revolution in Western thought brought about by the work of Charles Darwin (1809-82). Born in 1844 in Saxony, the son of a Lutheran pastor, his philosophy was influenced by his Protestant religious upbringing. Nietzsche's philosophical thought can be viewed as an attempt to find a new synthesis between Protestant Christianity (with its belief in the heroic individual) and classical paganism (with its worship of the power of nature).

Nietzsche was devastated by his cousins

MODERN MEANINGLESSNESS

★ Nietzsche, who even by the standards of highly strung philosophers had a sensitive disposition, took the intellectual consequences of Darwin's evolutionary theories seriously. The universe had not been made for humans by God, so humans were now alone in a universe without any real significance at all.

★ Nietzsche's whole philosophy can be seen as an attempt to answer this one question: *How do we live in world without something (a God) that guarantees that life has meaning?* In 1882 Nietzsche finally conceded that God is dead, and so began his long philosophical quest to find a non-religious answer to the "meaning of life" and to escape the feelings of despair that

DARWIN'S THEORY

Darwin claimed in *The Origin of Species* that humans, rather than being created in God's image, were the evolutionary cousins of monkeys and apes. For Nietzsche this was devastating news.

followed his loss of faith in Christianity. This condition, which he termed nihilism, the belief that everything is meaningless, was for Nietzsche the chief philosophical problem facing the modern world.

DIRE PREDICTIONS

* Nietzsche was one of the chief prophets of the modern age. He accurately predicted that life in the twentieth century would be a perilous time; in a world without God, people would follow anyone or anything that offered them some sense of personal worth in a universe increasingly perceived to be devoid of significance.
* Nietzsche warned of the dangers that lay in the future, but he harbored little faith in the moral abilities of the majority of "ordinary people." Unlike Marx, Nietzsche denied that any hope for a better future lay with the proletariat. Like many German philosophers, he was something of an elitist and perceived the bulk of humanity as being rather like cattle, a herd who follow a herd mentality.

KEY WORDS

EVOLUTION: Darwin's theory that all life forms have developed over a period of time from more primitive life forms

NIHILISM: the philosophical idea that there is no meaning in anything

THE PALE CRIMINAL

For Nietzsche, the twentieth century would be the age of the pale criminal, the false prophet who offers salvation but merely manipulates people to their doom. In light of the atrocities committed by Hitler and Stalin, this is a truly remarkable prediction.

Ha Ha what a laugh Ha Ha

THE ÜBERMENSCHEN

★ In contrast to the herd, there are, according to Nietzsche, a few "great men," *übermenschen*, who can rise above the bovine world of common folk. These men live according to their own values rather than following those imposed by others, and Nietzsche thought that we all should live like these great men and create our own values for ourselves. Nietzsche believed that his philosophy would save future humanity from the horrors of nihilism.

NIETZSCHE'S MADNESS

By the late 1880s, Nietzsche had started to believe that he was the first living example of an übermensch and, partly as a consequence, he started to crack up. He spent the last ten years of his life insane with only his mother to care for him.

AN ALTERNATIVE TO CHRISTIANITY

★ Nietzsche attempted to invent a new kind of life-affirming spirituality based on the worship of the Greek god of wine and intoxication—Dionysus. This form of spirituality would oppose the life-denying and otherworldly forms of Christian spirituality, which in his view, made people hate themselves and hate life. In fact the Christian worship of a dead God—the crucified Jesus—Nietzsche believed to be the major obstacle in the way of his attempt

we want wine

intoxication rules

to **"transvalue all values,"** to rethink the nature of morality so that a new ethic of art and life could be liberated from religion's deadly grasp.

NIETZSCHE'S BIBLE

★ Nietzsche increasingly came to see himself as a kind of **philosophical saint**, and he wrote the strange and aphoristic *Also Sprach Zarathustra* (1883–85) as a "new bible," an aestheticist's answer to the New Testament. In this book, Nietzsche tells the story of the hermit Zarathustra, who decides to "go down" from his mountain retreat into the world of ordinary mortals. He then decides to preach his new gospel, that man must be overcome and that we should all prepare for the imminent arrival of **the übermensch.**

A DANGEROUS CONCLUSION

★ Nietzsche's ideas are important because they point out that in a postreligious world there are no absolute values; therefore, if one is to avoid the abyss of nihilism, one must create some interesting values for oneself. However, his belief that he could do this without any regard for the rest of humanity suggests that anyone who attempts to turn art into life without taking reality into account is toying with their own sanity. His death in 1900 marked the end of philosophical romanticism.

searching for values in art

ART AS REDEMPTION

Nietzsche's philosophy states that in a world without God-given values, it is necessary to be creative and to invent new values and new ways of living. For Nietzsche then, the highest form of human life is art, and the great artist is the true savior of humanity. Nietzsche's philosophy is hence both egoistic, in that it values heroic individuals, and aestheticist, in that it values the artist's ability to create things from nothing.

you are toying with your sanity

a mad philosopher

ENDGAMES

★ The romantic movement in philosophy can be seen as part of a wider cultural reaction to the perceived social and psychological costs of technocratic modernization. The romantics bemoaned the losses that they thought had accompanied scientifically driven "progress," and they longed for a return to a world where people lived more "natural" lives in more stable and secure communities.

Romantic failure

Romanticism was a cultural failure, and its ideas have become associated in the popular imagination with images of mad philosophers, consumptive artists, and demonic despots. This is a shame, because romantic philosophical thought points out a profound truth about what life is like for most people in the modern world.

a demonic despot

THE SENSITIVE PSYCHE

★ **The romantics complained that the rational models of both the self** and the world proposed by the technocratic philosophers were SUPERFICIAL TRAVESTIES OF SELFHOOD, and they tried to construct alternative accounts of the human person that were more sensitive to the non-rational and emotive dimensions of the human psyche.

★ **For the nineteenth-century romantic philosophers, the fate of the modern individual was not a happy one.** Most modern individuals, according to the romantics, were condemned to live PROFOUNDLY UNSATISFYING LIVES. Nietzsche, for example, thought that life in modern technocratic societies was a life of

"filth and miserable ease," and he tried to show how modern individuals have become overdomesticated by **"advances"** in the social application of reason in the form of modern science and technology.

UNCONSCIOUS URGES

★ This idea became the central philosophical focus of one of the twentieth century's most significant intellectual figures, **Sigmund Freud** (1856–1939). Freud accepted the romantic critiques of modern society, but he believed that he had found a scientific way of dealing with them. For Freud, what was needed was a **new science** of the mind—**psychoanalysis**—that was more sensitive to hidden, irrational depths of the psyche. Freud believed that the rationalists and the empiricists had only offered models of the **conscious mind** (**ego**) and had ignored the existence of the **unconscious (id)**.

EGO:
the rational, conscious level of the mind

ID:
the irrational, unconscious level of the mind

PSYCHOANALYSIS:
the science of the unconscious mind

Freud

Freud

Freud thought that dreams were the "royal road" to understanding the unconscious. For him, the unconscious mind symbolically revealed itself to the conscious mind only through our dreams, fantasies, and wishes, and he claimed that because these are primarily sexual, then so is our unconscious.

what is the mind?

SIGMUND FREUD

Freud

★ Sigmund Freud was born in the Moravian town of Freiburg in 1856. He went on to study medicine in Vienna. While studying in Paris, he became influenced by the ideas of the French physician Charcot, especially his attempts to cure hysterical paralysis using hypnotism. Freud's encounter with Charcot led him away from medicine, and he began to wonder how the mind and the body might be related. Charcot's use of hypnosis seemed to suggest that physical illnesses could have an underlying psychological cause and could therefore be treated by psychological means.

WHAT IS THE MIND?

★ It was from Charcot that Freud developed his two most important ideas—that **psychological problems could be cured by the use of words**, and that **ideas, not underlying physical illness, could be the real causes of many physical and psychological illnesses**. Although Freud is now famous as a founding father of modern psychology, his ideas were also driven by philosophical concerns. The two main questions that guided Freud's subsequent psychological investigations were two of the biggest questions of the modern the world—*what is the mind, and how does it develop?*

modern illnesses are all in the mind

First interests

Freud's early medical research was concerned with the reproductive organs of eels. Some might say that this would account for his later preoccupations!

★ In 1895, while traveling on a train back from a conference in Berlin, Freud came up with the idea for a technocratic Project for a Scientific Psychology. In this work, Freud developed his idea of the mind as a self-regulating system whose purpose was the pleasurable discharge of energy. According to Freud, the mind is something like a cross between a thermostat and a pressure cooker in that it attempts to maintain itself at a steady state of psychic energy. For Freud, the human mind was thus a kind of **dynamic machine**.

KEY WORDS

THE UNCONSCIOUS: the part of the mind that pursues basic human desires
PLEASURE PRINCIPLE: the fundamental human need for gratification of basic desires
THE SUPEREGO: the part of the mind that embarrasses or shames us into controlling our basic desires and makes us civilized

THE UNCONSCIOUS

★ Freud used this idea to develop his theory of the unconscious. He believed that one of the most important sources of such psychic energy was the human instinct, such as the need for food or sex. These instincts were not under the control of the conscious or rational part of the mind. They were under the control of another, more fundamental part of the mind, the unconscious mind. This worked according to its own principle—**the pleasure principle**. For Freud, this unconscious mind demanded immediate pleasurable gratification, and it became very agitated if its pleasurable efforts were in any way thwarted.

the desires of the unconscious

A CONSTANT STRUGGLE

* The conscious mind very often finds basic impulses like hunger and sexual desire unacceptable or impossible to satisfy. As we all know, a sudden urge to eat or sleep can be both impractical and socially embarrassing. For Freud, the conscious mind constantly has to defend itself against a perpetual tide of unconscious desires, and the most significant way such unwanted ideas are dealt with is by repressing them. By this, Freud meant "sending them back to the unconscious."

satisfying basic impulses

KEEPING THINGS UNDER WRAPS

* However, such ideas are never simply forgotten. They demand satisfaction, and if there is no easy way of discharging them, they can only be satisfied by wishing that they were true. *This is presumably why hungry people dream about food, prisoners fantasize about escaping, and bachelor philosophers dream about beautiful goddesses.*

* This idea that our minds contain lots of repressed material that can affect how we think and act became the cornerstone of Freud's theory of psychological development. For Freud, young children's minds are driven purely by drives for pleasure, including, controversially, sexual pleasure. The task of parents is to civilize children into bringing these drives under rational and moral control.

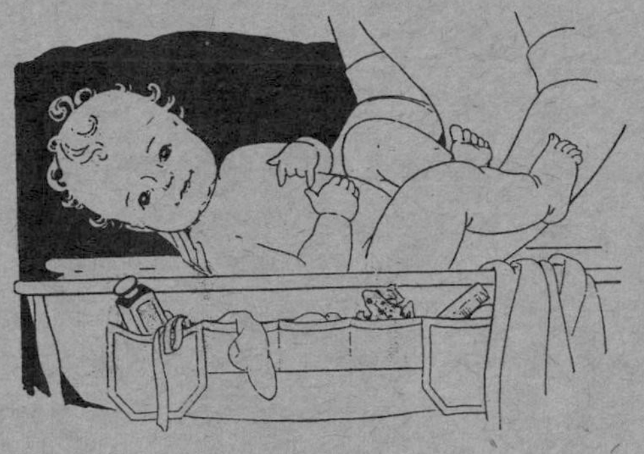

teaching children the values of control and civilization

KEEP IT CLEAN!

★ However, this is sometimes only achieved at great psychological expense to the child. For example, Freud believed that overzealous training of children to control their basic need to discharge feces could lead to "anally-fixated" adult personalities. If a child is made to think that defecating is dirty then he might try to defend himself against such desires to "make a mess." Such "anally retentive" people may turn out to be excessively tidy and, in some cases, mean and nasty individuals. But many subsequent psychologists think Freud was potty to blame it on the potty!

★ After World War I, Freud became increasingly depressed about human nature. In *Beyond the Pleasure Principle*, he argued that the unconscious was not simply motivated by pleasure, but was also driven by a basic desire for destruction. Freud gave this idea the rather macabre name **"the death drive"** and for him it represented a basic drive on the part of the unconscious mind to return to a state of blissful nonexistence.

Freud's last word

Late in his life Freud wrote his most explicitly philosophical work, *Civilisation and its Discontents.* In this work he argues that our most basic desires can never be satisfied, and that the Marxist idea of an ideal communist society is nothing more than a silly wish. In these later works he suggests that there is no easy way to live with our unconscious desires and that "every man must find out for himself in what particular fashion he can be saved." Thus, in the end, psychoanalysis became an odd kind of moral philosophy.

it's my basic desire for destruction

the death drive

I'm so unpredictable

ANIMAL INSTINCTS

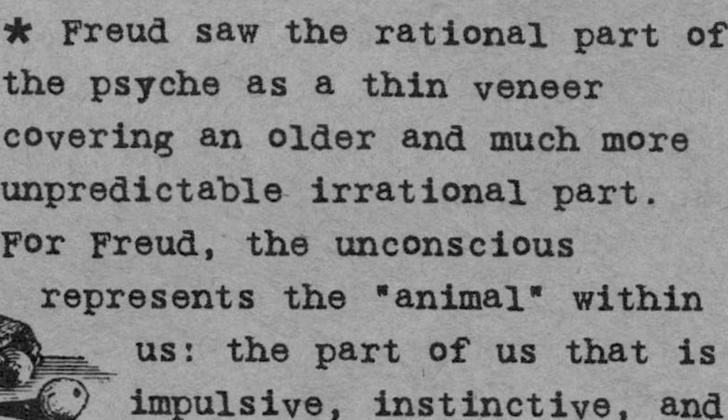

★ Freud saw the rational part of the psyche as a thin veneer covering an older and much more unpredictable irrational part. For Freud, the unconscious represents the "animal" within us: the part of us that is impulsive, instinctive, and demands immediate gratification.

the animal within us

THE DEMON WITHIN

★ Freud paints a picture of the human mind in conflict with itself and suggests that all we can hope for is to accept the "demon within us" and bring it under rational forms of control.

★ According to Freud, most people could only achieve this kind of self-mastery after years of therapy, conducted by a recognized **psychoanalyst**. For this reason, Freud was an arch-technocrat who believed that the most significant problems of human life could only ever be answered by psychological experts trained in the strange arts of psychoanalysis.

SCIENCE HAS THE ANSWER

Freud's ideas represent a technocratic answer to the problems raised by the nineteenth-century romantics. In fact, in the early part of the twentieth century, this was the trend of a lot of intellectual thinking, and many philosophers believed that science could meet all the difficulties of modern life that the romantics had identified.

PHENOMENOLOGY

★ The German philosopher **Edmund Husserl** (1859–1938) tried to develop a new science of **lived experience** that attempted to understand the specifics of human interpretation and judgement—

something the romantics had claimed was an art—in more abstract and rational ways. However, he never really succeeded in this task, and his new science of **phenomenology** never really took off.

FOCUS ON LANGUAGE

* At around the same time, an attempt to understand **language** in more rational ways also emerged. This kind of technocratic thinking about language can be found in the work **Gottlob Frege** (1848–1925). Frege thought that all meaningful human language could be reduced to logical formulas: abstract symbolic expressions that look something like algebra. Frege, in his attempts to systematize human language, opened the way for the modern science of language, linguistics. Frege's new philosophy of language would influence **Bertrand Russell** (1872–1970) and his pupil **Ludwig Wittgenstein** (1889–1951).

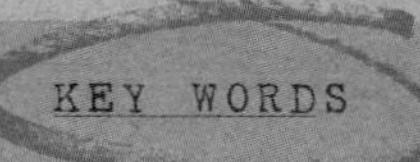

PSYCHOANALYST: self-proclaimed expert in the workings of the unconscious mind

PHENOMENOLOGY: the science of the conscious mind that attempts to understand how our minds make meanings

PHILOSOPHY OF LANGUAGE: the attempt to uncover the "logical structure" of all human languages

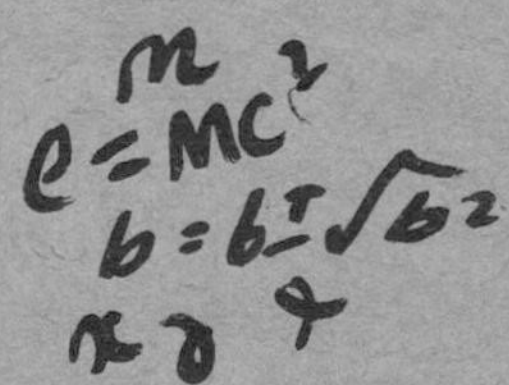

"what are numbers?"

a question hit Wittgenstein on the head

LUDWIG WITTGENSTEIN

* The story of Wittgenstein's introduction to philosophy is now very much part of philosophical folklore. He was studying engineering at Manchester University when he was suddenly struck by the question, "What are numbers?" He thought this was a much more interesting question than those typically found in engineering, but as he came to realize, it was also a much harder question to answer.

RUSSELL'S INFLUENCE

* Wittgenstein went to Cambridge and asked Bertrand Russell, the most famous mathematician of the age, whether he could answer this question for him. Russell told Wittgenstein to go away and write something on the subject. When Wittgenstein returned with his essay some months later, Russell was so impressed with his work that he urged him to become a philosopher, so Wittgenstein left Manchester and went to Cambridge to study under Russell.

* Russell influenced Wittgenstein greatly, and he became embroiled in the problems and issues in the philosophy of language that Frege and Russell were developing. This school of philosophy was concerned with the deep and puzzling question, "What makes language

"what makes language meaningful?"

are chickens fowl, or just a bit unfriendly?

FLYING A KITE

Wittgenstein's engineering work was in aeronautics and involved flying kites on a windy hill in northern England.

meaningful?" Philosophers of language usually spend a lot of their time wondering why, for example, the words "chicken" and "fries" mean what they do.

Wittgenstein, the philosopher at war

UNHAPPY FAMILIES

Wittgenstein's father was a wealthy Viennese steel magnate, and his childhood environment had all the trimmings that went with upper-class family life in the late Habsburg period. The Wittgenstein family was not a happy one, however. Two of his older brothers committed suicide, and Wittgenstein himself was troubled by depressive and suicidal feelings throughout his life.

WORDS AND WITTGENSTEIN

* The young Wittgenstein developed his own philosophical account of how words get their meaning. According to him, human language is meaningful because it represents reality as a picture does; that is, a sentence (or as philosophers are apt to say, **a proposition**) has sense if, and only if, it accurately depicts a possible state of affairs. This is sometimes called **the picture theory of meaning** and Wittgenstein revealed it to the world in the only book to be published in his lifetime, the *Tractatus Logico-philosophicus* (published in 1921).

A difficult book

Wittgenstein's *Tractatus Logico-philosophicus* was written in the trenches during World War I while Wittgenstein was serving as a volunteer in the Austrian army. It is one of the most obscure and difficult books in the history of philosophy.

ANOTHER TYPE OF ATOM

★ The picture theory of meaning claims that each proposition consists of simple elements that function like simple pictures, and that each of these language elements refers to a corresponding simple element, or "atom," in the world. Wittgenstein's early metaphysics is therefore sometimes called "logical atomism" in that it suggests that the world must be made up of simple basic "atoms" for language to be possible at all.

MEANINGLESS LANGUAGE

★ Most philosophers after Wittgenstein failed to find this at all convincing. First, they asked, "WHAT ON EARTH ARE THESE MYSTERIOUS ATOMS?" They are clearly not the same as the atoms referred to by physicists, because most of our common "propositions" refer to everyday things like chairs. If the sentence "THIS IS A CHAIR" functions like a picture, then what are we to take as the sentence's most simple elements—blobs of color perhaps, like in an impressionist painting?

★ Worse still, as Wittgenstein conceded, according to his theory of meaning most of what we say is simply meaningless because it doesn't depict anything. This is not only true of ethical and religious language, but of philosophical language as well.

this is a chair

School's out

After completing his book, Wittgenstein believed that he had solved all the problems of philosophy and went off to work as a primary-school teacher in Austria. However, things didn't work out and the parents of his pupils complained about his harsh treatment of their children. They eventually sued him for cruelty. Wittgenstein left teaching and ran back to Cambridge.

Wittgenstein was a mean teacher and was later sued for cruelty

THE REVISIONIST

* While on a train journey with the Italian economist Piero Sraffa, Wittgenstein decided to explain the picture theory. In response, Sraffa made a rude Italian gesture and asked what it was meant to be a picture of. Wittgenstein was lost for words. Sraffa had shown Wittgenstein that **language was cultural and not simply propositional**. He was now convinced that any philosophy must start from the premise that human meaning is not simply a matter of some kind of metaphysical correspondence between language and the world, but is **a product of culture and society**.

* Wittgenstein began to reconsider his earlier philosophy, and it slowly dawned on him that as a young man his philosophical views had been a little odd, to say the least.

A philosophical ladder

Wittgenstein accepted that his own philosophy was literally meaningless. He stated at the end of the *Tractatus* that his philosophy was more like useful nonsense, a ladder that you must discard once you have used it to climb to a higher plane. In this sense, the early Wittgenstein was something of a mystical neoplatonist.

philosophy is like a ladder that can be used then discarded

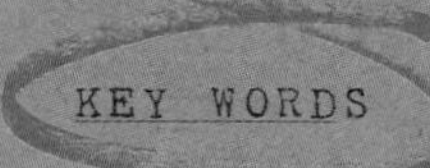

LOGICAL ATOMISM: theory of language that says that the world is made up of simple basic atoms which we use words to describe

LANGUAGE GAMES

★ Wittgenstein's new philosophy viewed the basic elements of language as being more like games than pictures. He now became increasingly aware that, for most ordinary folk, language is a tool of social interaction—different kinds of words doing different kinds of jobs in the playful ebb and flow of ordinary social life. This gave the mature Wittgenstein the idea that language is made up of lots of language games. Therefore, the meaning of any word is the job that it does in the particular language game in which it is used.

USING WORDS

The meaning of the word "time" is determined by how it is used in the many and various everyday social activities in which it can be used. If you can use this word correctly in the appropriate context, then you know its meaning. Hence there are lots of different meanings to the word "time." For example, the word "time" in the question, "Do you remember a time when?" has a very different meaning from the word "time" in the question, "What time is it?"

A GAME WE CAN ALL PLAY

★ What did Wittgenstein mean by the term **"language game?"** Well, according to Wittgenstein, human life is made up of many different types of cultural activity: counting, describing, telling the time, getting ready to go out on a Friday night after work, etc.

★ For Wittgenstein, the meaning of a word is the role that it plays in a particular social activity. So there is no such thing as the meaning of a word. ***Meaning depends on use, and words tend to have a variety of different uses.*** So clearly, anybody who asks the question, "WHAT IS TIME?" is asking themselves a very misleading question, and they have failed to understand how human language works.

THE SICK PHILOSOPHERS

* Wittgenstein assumed that some people think that underneath all the different senses of ordinary words there must lie a common essential meaning. Wittgenstein thought that this was a fundamentally mistaken way of looking at the matter, a mistake typically made by philosophers.

Wittgenstein labeled philosophers as sick

* For the later Wittgenstein, philosophical problems stem not from wonder, but from a **bewitchment of the intelligence by means of language**. Philosophers forget that words have a *multiplicity of meanings*, and so they search, like **Aristotle** did, for a metaphysical essence to particular concepts. This tendency, Wittgenstein thought, is a bit like a **sickness**, one which philosophers must be cured of if they were to see the world correctly. His opinion that philosophers are sick and that there is nothing beyond the "business" of everyday life makes the later Wittgenstein a bit of philistine.

most people only use language as a tool of social interaction

AN ODD PHILOSOPHER

Wittgenstein was one of the most remarkable and eccentric of philosophers. He was very rich but gave away all his money, lived for long periods in a hut in Norway, and was often seen eating pies in the front row at the cinema.

the business of everyday life

SLIPPERY STATEMENTS

Sartre

★ Both Russell and the early Wittgenstein claimed that unless you could reveal the logical structure inherent in any statement (or proposition, as these philosophers called them), then that statement was bereft of any meaning.

Kafka

KEY WORDS

EMOTIVISM: the idea that moral words like "good" are really just meaningless expressions of emotion, like "yipee!"

EXISTENTIALISM: romantic philosophy that claims that people are free beings, not technocratic "particles in force fields"

EXISTENTIALIST HERO person who accepts responsibility for his freedom

EMPTY WORDS

★ These early analytical philosophers (so-called because they believed that philosophical problems could be reduced to a logical analysis of language) thought that even though large parts of our language appear meaningful, the words, when analyzed logically, are more like empty gestures. For example, the **emotivists** claimed that words like "good" and "bad" don't refer to anything at all but function more like the emotional expressions "hurrah" and "boo."

PHILOSOPHERS' REFUGE

★ **As these new philosophies increasingly encroached** on romantic philosophical territory, those with romantic temperaments fled philosophy and tried to find refuge in art. The first half of the twentieth century saw the emergence of distinctly philosophical forms of art, especially the **philosophical novel**. This type of novel was concerned with the deeply morally ambiguous nature of modern existence and the difficulties that a now profoundly alone and powerless individual faced in his day to day dealings with others.

Josef K. under arrest

KAFKA'S X-FILES

★ In Franz Kafka's famous novel *The Trial*, Kafka tells the story of Josef K. who is arrested one morning for no apparent reason and told he is guilty of some charge. In order to prove his innocence, he has to find out first what he is being accused of, and this means dealing with a paranoia-inducing modern bureaucratic legal system. Kafka's novel thus deals with the dark side of modernity: how individuals can be terrorized by modern bureaucracies and made to feel guilty just for being alive.

GLOOMY TALES

Existentialist novels like those of Sartre and Kafka usually tell the story of an existential hero who single-handedly confronts the meaninglessness and absurdity of modern existence.

Freedom and guilt

In Sartre's most famous philosophical novel, *Nausea* (1938), Sartre's antihero Roquentin wonders how life can be made meaningful without appealing to the existence of a God. He comes to the conclusion that what life without God really means is that we all have a responsibility to use our godless freedom to make life meaningful. But as our own free choices inevitably harm others, this means that free choice always involves feelings of guilt and remorse.

MODERN PESSIMISM

* This tension between freedom and morality underlies much of Sartre's early writings, which means that he, along with Kafka, can be seen as addressing the religious issues of guilt and the possibility of redemption in a new modern context.

this is the rule, well for today anyway

Believe whatever is useful

Pragmatist ideas influenced the contemporary American philosopher **Willard van Orman Quine** (1908). He argued that if we found it useful, we should give up believing in such cherished truths as "1+1=2." Hence, all truths are revisable and, unlike diamonds, no knowledge is forever.

SOCIAL HELL

* Both **Sartre** and **Kafka** are essentially pessimistic about the modern world's power to redeem individuals from this overwhelming sense of guilt that, in a scientific age that DENIES THE REALITY OF HUMAN FREEDOM AND RESPONSIBILITY, has no apparent cause. To **Sartre**, the modern world is a kind of social hell where people hurt each other for no apparent reason and misunderstand each other most of the time.

THE ANTIPHILOSOPHICAL PHILOSOPHY

✱ The retreat of philosophy into art and radical politics allowed the philistines to develop their own "philosophies." In fact, the twentieth century has witnessed an explosion of various types of thinking that have, somewhat paradoxically, attempted to provide "PHILOSOPHICAL" justifications for the philistine's antiphilosophical views.

AMERICAN PRAGMATISTS

✱ Foremost among these new philosophies were the ideas of the AMERICAN PRAGMATISTS, **Charles Pierce** (1839–1914), **William James** (1842–1910), and **John Dewey** (1859–1952). They argued that all these arcane philosophical arguments about the true nature of reality and whether we can know about it were essentially **pointless** and that, if you spend too long thinking about the nature of reality, it is likely to "DRIVE YOU NUTS."

✱ Their solution was to reconceive our idea of truth in terms of **usefulness** rather than, as it had traditionally been understood by philosophers, a **correspondence with the world**. So for the pragmatists, a statement such as, say, "THIS CHAIR IS MADE UP OF ATOMS," is true, not because this chair is actually made of atoms but because it is useful to us to see the chair in this particular way.

PRAGMATISM:
the idea that "truth" is the most useful idea of the moment

what an interesting conversation

Relative truth

The contemporary pragmatist Richard Rorty (1931–) argues, like his philistine forefather Protagoras (see page 57), that all truths are relative and that culture is the measure of all things. However, for Rorty, it is American culture against which all other things get measured. According to Rorty, there is no such thing as philosophical truth but only more or less interesting "conversations." The most interesting conversation of all time is the polite conversation that respectable white "westerners" have been having with themselves, something Rorty calls **bourgeois liberalism**.

WILLIAM JAMES

★ William James became famous as both a psychologist and a philosopher, and in his first book, *The Principles of Psychology*, he advocates the idea, later to become popularized by the novelists James Joyce and Virginia Woolf, that the mind consists of separate streams of consciousness. According to him, the stream of thoughts that runs through the human mind is a bit like Heraclitus' river, in that nobody ever really has the same thoughts twice. For James, each thought is unique and can only be accessed by introspection.

William James

KEY WORDS

RADICAL EMPIRICISM: the metaphysical idea, similar to solipsism, that the universe is made up of "pure experience"

CASH VALUE: the idea that the significance of an idea lies in its "marketability"

PANPSYCHISM: the mystical idea that there is no distinction between mind and matter and that matter is itself conscious

NEW METAPHYSICS

★ James used this idea to form the basis of a new metaphysics that has been the most popular American variety of metaphysics ever since—**radical empiricism**. According to this idea, the fundamental stuff of the universe isn't mind or matter but something in-between, which he termed **pure experience**. With James, this idea took a decidedly religious turn, in that he seemed to suggest that the entire universe is in some sense conscious, a view that has become known as **panpsychism**. According to panpsychists, even molecules and Snickers bars are to some extent conscious, albeit less so than humans.

if you can sell it, it's a good idea

MEANING AND MONEY

* James became famous for his philosophical defense of pragmatism. For him the meaning or significance of any idea is something that he termed its **cash value**. Why did he equate meaning and cash? Cynics say that this was because he charged exorbitant prices to listen to his lectures, as the sophists did earlier.

* James also put forward the idea that the truth of any statement was to be found in its utility or usefulness. *According to him, we should give up believing in the truth of an idea—for instance, that killing people is wrong—if we no longer find the idea useful.* Conversely, if an idea "ain't broke," then "don't fix it." Some would say that his ideas have provided philosophical justifications for the habit of modern politicians of saying whatever is merely expedient.

EARLY DAYS

William James was born in New York in 1842. His father, Henry James Sr., was a religious mystic; William and his brother Henry Jr. (who was later to become a famous novelist) grew up in an intensely philosophical environment.

Talk Sense

However, James' pragmatism did have some positive influences. James was writing at a time when the infinite complexities of German idealism (especially Hegelian) held sway. These philosophical ideas were about as far removed from the everyday concerns of ordinary people as Pluto from Pittsburgh. James' response to the German idealists was "Damn the absolute!" James wanted to develop a more down-to-earth philosophy, but he allowed his obvious philosophical abilities to be corrupted by worldly considerations.

THE POSTMODERNISTS

★ Richard Rorty is also part of another philistine-led philosophical movement, postmodernism. This movement has its roots in the ideas of the radical architects of the early 1970s who rebelled against the coldly rational, abstract, and machinelike nature of most modern architecture. The postmodernists objected to modernist architects like Le Corbusier who claimed that architecture should be about aiding and abetting the technocrats in their utopian attempts to produce more "rational" and organized ways of life.

THE VOICE OF THE PEOPLE

★ The **postmodernists** claimed that **architecture** should not be about "EXPERT" architects and planners imposing their rational designs on an unsuspecting population, but should instead include in its designs the **needs and desires of those who people who actually have to live in these buildings**. Postmodern architects thus attempt to show a SENSITIVITY to local

KEY WORDS

POSTMODERNISM: contemporary philosophical movement that champions difference and variety over uniformity

METANARRATIVE: big, "all-encompassing" story that claims to be able to describe and explain everything (for example, science and religion)

DIFFERENCE: postmodern idea that the good life means recognizing the specific uniqueness of all things

cultures and traditions in their designs, and they celebrate the everyday world of popular reality over the dour rationality of science and technology.

SMALL IDEAS MATTER

* However, this rather nice idea of including the small ideas of ordinary people in the architectural design process gets transformed in the hands of so-called postmodern philosophers such as **Jean-Francois Lyotard** (1924–) into the crass suggestion that the only ideas that really matter are small ideas. Lyotard takes issue with the entire philosophical tradition and suggests that philosophy has been governed by the need to **construct big stories** of what the world is really like.

* These big stories (or, as he calls them, **metanarratives**), like those centered on notions of reason, progress, god, art, etc., try to provide philosophical answers for all people of whatever culture. This, Lyotard believes, is impossible (without recourse to some kind of conceptual "violence"), as the world is, in reality, a place where things and people are **different**.

BANNING BIG STORIES

* Lyotard thus objects that the very asking of big questions assumes that there are universal concerns. He refutes this and claims that the attempt to fit everyone into universal answers given to these big questions is tantamount to totalitarianism.

Lyotard says life is all about little stories

Small is beautiful

Against big questions and stories, Lyotard argues that life should be about little questions and little stories (*petit recits*). In the end, therefore, Lyotard comes close to suggesting that the meaning of life is to be found in gossip, and that the ideal form of human organization is a church tea party.

DERRIDA DECONSTRUCTS PHILOSOPHY

* Another postmodernist is the mysterious French philosopher Jacques Derrida (1930–). He again objects to the whole philosophical tradition and complains that it suffers from what he terms logocentrism.

creative deconstruction

Jacques Crusoe

Derrida seems to be a Crusoe-like philosophical figure, marooned on Aporia Island, waiting for the good ship Philosophical Speculation to rescue him. In his recent work, he has claimed that our most basic ideas about justice **cannot** be deconstructed and so maybe his newfound moral certainty will provide a raft for his escape.

LOGOCENTRISM

* What he means by this is that philosophy has tended to assume that there is some general ultimate purpose or direction to both the cosmos and human history, and that the purpose can be ascertained by means of QUIET PHILOSOPHICAL REFLECTION. He argues that we need to **deconstruct this idea** and show that any attempt to state the origin and purpose of the cosmos and human history necessarily conceals as much truth as it reveals.

* For example, Marx's idea that the ultimate purpose of human history was communism has nothing to say about the role of women in this society or how issues of race or sexuality might resolve themselves. Derrida's philosophy is, then, an attempt to read the grand philosophical texts, not for what is there, but for what is *not* there

and so liberate philosophical thought from the horrors of "MASCULINISM" (male-centered thinking) and "EUROCENTRISM" (European-centered thinking).

* There is much to be commended here, and Derrida does raise some important questions. However, until recently, he has never made any positive philosophical contributions of his own. He seems content to undermine the philosophical tradition without saying anything about the ways of thinking that might take its place. So though there is something of the philosopher in Derrida, in that he seems prepared to ask the most difficult and fundamental of all philosophical questions—the question "WHAT IS PHILOSOPHY?"—he never seems to find a way out of his own **aporias** (see page 58).

THE OBSOLESCENCE OF PHILOSOPHY

* The story of twentieth-century philosophy is thus a story of the **disappearance** of philosophy. Philosophical questions increasingly find themselves translated into scientific and practical questions. So, for example, in the hands of the technocrats, the question, "WHAT IS TIME?" becomes a question for advanced physics. In the hands of the philistines, it becomes translated into the practical question, "HOW MUCH TIME HAVE I GOT?" In such a cultural climate, it might be asked how philosophy can survive.

PHILOSOPHY IS DEAD?

Since many philosophers think that philosophical speculation is an essentially pointless activity, it is not surprising that philosophers are no longer taken seriously. Most people would agree that true philosophical speculation can now only be found in art and poetry.

HEIDEGGER'S BEING

★ There are some notable exceptions to this trend toward abandoning philosophy. One of the most important philosophers (in the truest sense of the word) this century was Martin Heidegger (1889-1976).

is it genuine?

why does a natural tomato appear more real than a high-tech one?

KEY WORDS

BEING:
the true "isness" that resides in all things

DASEIN:
the strange nature of human "isness" that enables us to exist for ourselves in space (here) and time (now)

AUTHENTICITY:
the appearance of true "isness"; for us this means recognizing the reality of our dasein: death

THE REAL THING

★ Heidegger complained that with the rise of modern technological civilization we have made the fatal error of mistaking the artificial world produced by science and technology for the real thing. According to Heidegger, we have forgotten Being. Although it is extremely hard to pin down exactly what Heidegger meant by this, if we use an analogy we might just get there.

★ **Why do we prefer natural, organically grown food to, say, irradiated and genetically engineered food?** Well, assuming that they are both equally safe, some of us still feel that the NATURAL TOMATO IS SOMEHOW MORE REAL THAN THE TECHNOLOGICALLY MANUFACTURED VARIETY. Why? It is hard to say. They might even look and taste identical, but we think that the former is simply more **authentic** than the latter. This, in some sense, captures what Heidegger means by Being.

THE TWO TYPES

* Being, for Heidegger, is what **authentic** human beings are in touch with, but what **inauthentic** people have forgotten. Inauthentic types (*der Mann*) are, according to Heidegger, happy to "go with the flow" of modern life without ever really concerning themselves with any of the deeper questions about the nature and purpose of their existence.

DEATH AND BEING

* AUTHENTICITY, FOR HEIDEGGER, stems from an awareness of our finitude, and an awareness of death leads one to consider the big questions about the purpose of existence. It is through an **awareness of death** that we come to appreciate the reality of our own **being there** (*dasein*), and we become aware that BEING reveals itself through our own authentic actions.

* For some people, this type of AUTHENTIC EXISTENTIAL AWARENESS only emerges toward the end of life, and very often this is too late. Heidegger's philosophy thus recaptures something of the original spirit of the early pre-Socratic philosophers, and he tries to reinstate something of their original sense of wonder about the nature and purpose of existence.

DUBIOUS POLITICS

During the 1930s, Heidegger joined the Nazi party, and his reputation has never really recovered. After the defeat of the Nazis in 1945, he never renounced his Nazism, leading some to claim that he displays the worst excesses of romantic thinking.

death is the handle to life

freeing Freud's ideas

THE FRANKFURT SCHOOL

* Heidegger influenced two other philosophers who were also to have a profound effect on the future direction of philosophical thought. Herbert Marcuse (1898-1979), who was a member of the Frankfurt School, attempted to combine Heidegger's ideas with those of Freud, thus attempting to liberate Freud's ideas from their imprisonment in technocratic rationalism.

KEY WORDS

CRITICAL THEORIES: philosophies that claim the world could be much better than it is

NEGATIVE THINKING: any way of thinking that states we can never really know what we want but that we can know what we don't want

LIVING IN A CAGE

* The FRANKFURT SCHOOL were a group of ***Jewish intellectuals*** who fled the Nazis to find a better life in the United States. They agreed with sociologist **Max Weber** that the modern world was a bureaucratic "IRON CAGE."

* **In his book *Eros and Civilisation* (1955), Marcuse agrees** with Heidegger that modern technocratic society is an organized system of non-Being. This, for Marcuse, could be understood in essentially psychoanalytic terms as an expression of the **unconscious death drive**. For Marcuse therefore, modern societies are driven by an unconscious need on the part of those who control them to return everything to a state of

nothingness, and their so-called reason and rationality is just a disguised way of controlling the erotic forces of life.

ACCENTUATE THE NEGATIVE

★ Marcuse's ideas led some people to reject society altogether. It is now widely accepted that dropping out of society with no clear idea of the alternatives to that society was a very bad idea indeed. This goes to show that unless **critical** philosophies like Marcuse's are guided by a strong sense of the ethical, they can easily collapse into a purely negative philosophy that denies that there is anything beyond the horizon of modern technocratic societies. This was the fate of his friend and Frankfurt School colleague **Theodor Adorno** (1903–69)—more on him on page 172.

THE ROLE OF THE OUTCAST

★ **Michel Foucault** (see pages 176–79) takes these ideas into the realm of practical politics. He claims that we should resist modern forms of technocratic power, which has the discipline and control of its subjects as its central concern. We should allow those excluded from the rational order of modern technocracy—the insane, the criminal, and the sexually deviant—to have their say. Foucault's philosophy thus represents a celebration of those who live at the margins of modernity.

Hippie culture

Marcuse's ideas influenced those 1960s radicals who opposed the war in Vietnam, espoused "free love," and advised everyone to "drop out" of mainstream society.

turn on, tune in, and drop out

Scandal

With Foucault, philosophy degenerates into an orgy of self-destruction. Rather than accept the routines of modern technocratic life, philosophy celebrates debauchery: sex, drugs, and rock and roll become the alternative authentic ethics to those espoused by the technocrats.

there is no positive image of the future

Adorno's nightmare

AUTHORITARIAN PERSONALITIES: bossy, authority-loving sado-masochists who love their bosses and revile their "inferiors"

CULTURAL INDUSTRIES: modern industries, such as entertainment and fashion, dedicated to selling culture at a profit

THEODOR ADORNO

The key to understanding Adorno's philosophy is his perceived "Jewishness." Like many other radical Jewish intellectuals, he was attracted to Marxist philosophy, and with his friend Max Horkheimer, he set up the Frankfurt School for social research in 1923. This school tried to blend Marxist philosophy and Freudian psychology into a critical theory of society.

WHAT'S GONE WRONG?

* The Frankfurt School's theory would attempt to reveal the inherent social contradictions at the heart of modern societies. In particular, they wanted to explain the contradiction between what modern societies promised (such as **life, liberty, and happiness**) and what they actually delivered (**something altogether more unpleasant**). Like many left-wing German intellectuals, Adorno fully expected a more free and just society to emerge from the economic ruins of 1930s Germany. However, the growth of Nazism both shocked and horrified him. How could such a political evil happen in modern times?

* For Adorno, the only explanation for the rise of Fascism was that the majority

(mass) of people living in modern societies are both psychologically damaged and manipulated by powerful leaders and institutions. According to Adorno, Fascism has its root cause in something that he termed the **authoritarian personality**. Such people, because of their harsh repressive childhood, admire the powerful and detest the weak and the "deviant." These pathological feelings of hatred are easily manipulated by powerful orators such as Hitler. They become directed toward specific minority social groups like gays, gypsies, and Jews.

A cultured childhood

Adorno was born Theodor Wisengrund, in Frankfurt, Germany, in 1903. His father was a wealthy Jewish wine merchant and his early childhood years were, by all accounts, intellectually stimulating. He spent his formative years reading Kant and playing difficult Beethoven sonatas to admiring family audiences.

THE PROBLEM OF CULTURE

* *Adorno thought that the basic problem of the modern world was the problem of culture.* Modern ways of life were fundamentally different from the cultures of the past. While traditional cultures provided people with a sense of significance and their "place in the world," modern cultures were now largely about escaping from the endless toil of the rat race. Thus, for Adorno, culture in modern times no longer provided meaning and purpose to people's lives.

Adorno's cultured upbringing

CULTURAL HABITS

★ Adorno was horrified by the cultural lives of postwar Westerners. He thought that sitting at home watching television or listening to Elvis was a travesty of culture. Modern individuals had allowed themselves to become "manipulated" by the modern bureaucratic state and what he termed "the cultural industries": pop music, news media, and advertising. In fact he viewed these as being not much better than Nazi propaganda in their manipulative effects.

KEY WORDS

NEGATIVE DIALECTICS: Adorno's term for the way of "not-thinking" forced on philosophy by the horrors of Auschwitz

POP CULTURE VS. HIGH CULTURE

★ What kinds of activity did Adorno think were still culturally significant? Well, Adorno thought that only high culture, in particular German philosophy and classical music, retained any value in a world increasingly governed by an all-powerful technocratic system. As a consequence, Adorno is very often perceived an elitist philosopher—a cultural "snob" who "looked down his nose" at the everyday world. Ironically, this made him little better than the technocrats he opposed.

the dead hand of Western culture

AFTER THE HOLOCAUST

★ However, there was more to Adorno's thought than this. After World War II, he returned from the US, where he had helped set up the New School for Social Research in New York, to his native Germany. There he began to contemplate the nature and significance of the Holocaust. Adorno thought that the Holocaust signified the ultimate power of the technocratic system over a helpless humanity and he became increasingly depressed about humanity's future. **"No poetry after Auschwitz"** was one of his most famous aphorisms to emerge from this period, and his philosophy became more significantly influenced by Judaism.

"there can be no poetry after Auschwitz"

THE HORRORS OF MODERNITY

★ *For Adorno, the modern world after Auschwitz was one of such utter barbarity that it simply could not be understood. It could only be negated. Adorno's later philosophy is thus the opposite of Parmenides'. After Auschwitz, the way of "it is" has been barred.* The only possible way for thought is the way of "it is not," which as we have seen is the way of not-thinking or, to use his terminology, **negative dialectics**. No positive image of the future could be constructed out of the present and, as a result, critical theory has often been given the title **the melancholy science**. Adorno is finally left waiting for a Messiah to free us from the horrors of modernity and, to this extent, critical theory finally collapsed into Judaism.

An influential philosopher

Adorno's influence on later philosophers has been immense. Though modern empiricists claim that his philosophy is nothing more than common sense dressed up in high-sounding language, his ideas have been championed by some recent postmodern philosophers who find his critique of modernity both powerful and appealing. We are perhaps still too close to Adorno to ascertain the true worth of his philosophy. He died in 1967.

Oppressive reason

Foucault tried to show, via careful historical analysis, that the modern world, although superficially more civilized than its medieval predecessor, was built on a new and more extensive type of cruelty—the oppression of those who failed to comply with new authority of reason. Foucault saw the modern world as one that excluded women, artists, the insane, the "criminal," and virtually anybody else who simply didn't "fit in" to the new rational, secular order.

RADICALISM

Foucault was politically active throughout his life, and he, along with many other French intellectuals, was involved in the left-wing political movements of the 1960s. Following the defeat of these movements after the student-led disturbances in Paris in May 1968, Foucault became disillusioned with orthodox Marxist philosophy.

MICHEL FOUCAULT

★ Michel Foucault was born in France in 1926. His ideas represent a radical critique of the modern technocratic social order, and his philosophy can be viewed as being similar to Marxism (see pages 134-37) in its attempt to point to more a just and humane form of modern society.

Foucault saw the modern world as one that excluded women

THE NATURE OF POWER

★ Although modern philosophers had claimed that their rationalist philosophies allowed humanity to be liberated from its irrational past, **Foucault** argued that the modern world was in reality a **great confinement** where instead of freeing individuals, rationality actually trapped them inside a new, more insidious power structure.

★ The major philosophical questions that underpinned his histories (or, as he termed them, **archaeologies**) were the questions, "WHAT IS POWER?" and, "HOW DOES POWER OPERATE IN MODERN SOCIETIES?" This makes Foucault a **political philosopher**, though many of his ideas raise important questions about **ethics**.

BUREAUCRATIC POWER

* In Foucault's early works, he argued that POWER IS A PRODUCT OF THE GAZE. **Power, for Foucault, was the ability to make the invisible visible,** and modern forms of power still operate according to this principle. Modern bureaucratic systems have to categorize, measure, diagnose, and appraise particular "MARGINAL" social groups in order to keep society functioning in an organized way.

MEDICAL CONTROL

* In *Madness and Civilization* (1965) and *The Birth of the Clinic*, **he tried to show how little the emergence of medical science had to do with scientific truth**. He claimed that medicine was really about the control and confinement of the insane and the generally deviant, and that modern "CIVILIZATION" had been built on this kind of medical control of individuals.

* In *Discipline and Punish* (1977), Foucault elaborated on this basic theme and tried to show how modern forms of punishment, like prison, involved the exercise of an excessive form of modern power.

POWER:
ability to categorize and hence control others; this power belongs to **the gazer** who compels others to see in the way that he sees

Everyone's looking at me

Modern power, for Foucault, works something like the gaze of the prison officers in **Bentham's panopticon** (see page 119), in that everyone is subject to it but nobody is aware of it. For Foucault, power is everywhere and we can't see it. This has led some critics to claim that he was more than a little paranoid.

categorize, measure, diagnose, and appraise

THE PRESSURE TO CONFORM

★ Foucault paints a dark picture of modern life. For him, modernity is like a prison without any bars. The bars exist inside our heads, and they have been placed there by the various modern institutions that we pass through during the course of our lives, in particular, the family, the school, and the workplace.

our self-inflicted prison

RESISTING POWER

free spirits are bashed into shape

★ Modern technocratic society, for Foucault, rather than being based on greater individual freedom as its apologists suggest, is in fact a disciplinary society that exerts its controlling influence through instilling guilt, shame, and a general sense of "abnormality" in those who so much as entertain the idea of transgressing its norms. Those that carry through such ideas are removed from society so that they can be suitably "refashioned" and returned "fully recovered" from their "illness."

★ Foucault, at times, seems to suggest that there is nothing that we can do about this and some commentators therefore see his philosophy as deeply **cynical**. However, he also urges us not to succumb to despair and that those

living under modern technocratic systems have to be made aware that they are **a lot more free than they feel they are**. In his later work, Foucault urges us to resist modern forms of power and refuse to submit to the diagnostic examinations that modern systems force on us. The fact that he is prepared to ask the question, "How is individual freedom possible in the modern world?" makes him a **moral** as well as a **political philosopher**.

refuse to submit to diagnostic examinations

RESISTING TECHNOCRACY

* Foucault's philosophy was not simply academic. He tried to resist the disciplinary power of modern technocracy and lived the life of a PLEASURE-SEEKING PLAYBOY. Some recent thinkers claim that, as Foucault tried to resist the modern world by *turning his life into a work of art*, his philosophy really champions the values of **art. Hence he** should not be viewed as kind of contemporary "Marx" extolling the values of freedom and justice.
* Foucault did try to live his philosophy, and this makes him one of the modern world's true philosophers. However, the moral of Foucault's self-destructive life is that anyone who tries to turn the values of art into life is bound to come to grief on the rocks of pleasurable excess.

A campaigning philosopher

Foucault campaigned for the rights of prisoners and children and was a key figure in gay politics. However, with Foucault, as with many contemporary French intellectuals, it is hard to see where fashion ends and real life begins.

resisting the power of the modern technocracy

CHAPTER 7

IT'S A WONDERFUL LIFE?

★ Well, what did you make of the story? Some philosophers might argue that the story told here is nothing more than a crude attempt to popularize ideas that should not or cannot be popularized. They might complain that the narrator is a vulgar philosopher who fails to treat the sacred canon of philosophical ideas with sufficient respect.

A pointless game

Philosophy, as it is taught in mainstream universities, says nothing to students about the big questions of their lives. In these places, philosophy has become a tired and pointless academic game, a bit like an over-intellectualized game of I-spy in which the aim is to spot the logical fallacy in some philosopher's argument.

I spy...

...with my little eye

THE ACADEMIC WORLD

★ However, people who hold such views are increasingly perceived, with some justification, to be philosophy's problem.

★ They are philosophical **"fuddy duddies"** who claim that, in the world of philosophy, everything "HAPPENS AS IT SHOULD HAPPEN" in the *"best of all philosophical worlds."* But this view simply cannot be sustained for much longer. The kind of philosophy studied at university is mostly a matter of becoming trained in the arcane art of "formal logic."

★ Unless philosophy can begin saying something about our ordinary everyday lives, then it does not deserve the respect it so craves. Many German philosophers, like **Adorno**, claimed that philosophy should remain the privilege of an elite few and should not be allowed to fall into the quotidian or everyday existence. But what is there to be scared of? Is this just another misplaced aristocratic fear of the *hoi polloi*?

Get A Grip On Philosophy is a great book and it's on the reading list

PHILOSOPHY'S IVORY TOWER

* The fact that (for most people) the experience of studying philosophy—in Britain and North America at least—is a purely routine exercise, more like manually operating a type of "grinding machine," is clearly an important factor in philosophy's current demise. This type of "analytical philosophy" has allowed itself to be seduced by the alluring power of logical analysis and other philosophical techniques, and, as a consequence, **philosophy has alienated itself from the source of its speculative energies.**

* Philosophy has become too timid and unprepared to ask the big and challenging questions of life. It has lost touch with the everyday world, and so it is seen as being divorced from real concerns and exhibiting the worst excesses of academic detachment.

ENGAGED PHILOSOPHERS

Philosophers of the past tried seriously to address the big questions of their time. For all his faults, at least Bertrand Russell was prepared to stand up for his beliefs (he was jailed as a conscientious objector during World War I) and Marx, Sartre, and Foucault tried to develop philosophies that enabled them to **engage** with their worlds.

is philosophy relevant?

A MIRROR ON PHILOSOPHY

* To this extent, philosophy, as an approach to understanding the world, is in crisis; if this crisis is not addressed quickly, then we may witness the marginalization of philosophy, in pretty much the same way that we have witnessed the cultural marginalization of theology or classical history. The effect of this would be to close forever the window that philosophy opened—a window that allows us to ask the big questions in nontechnical and non-common-sense ways.

THE OLD GUARD

* The old guard of philosophical conservatives want to hold on to the traditional ways of doing philosophy—essentially authoritarian and "technocratic" views of the nature of philosophy that have their roots in the ideas of **Plato** and **Aristotle**. They do not seem to realize that it is precisely contemporary philosophy's failure to capture the popular imagination that is, perhaps, the major causal factor behind its long-term relative cultural decline.

* *As long as the big questions of life remain in the hands of the technocrats and philistines of this world, philosophy seems doomed to suffer a slow death from its own self-imposed irrelevance.*

this mirror needs resilvering

✱ Because of this, those of us who love philosophy need to look closely at the **practice of philosophy**, the way it is taught, researched, and popularly represented, if we want to find a truer diagnosis and prognosis of its current illnesses.

we're ready for you, Mr. Philosophy

How philosophy can win friends

I would suggest that philosophy needs to turn full circle and return to its prephilosophical roots. This means rethinking and reevaluating the ideas of the pre-Socratics. They managed to combine the enchantment of Pagan cultures with the sober curiosity of the rational temperament. For them, philosophy was a wonderful way to understand the world, and philosophy needs to rediscover this original sense of wonder.

back to basics

QUESTIONS FOR PHILOSOPHY NOW

✱ The tough questions are: can philosophy recover? Will making philosophy more widely popular aid its recovery? How do we make philosophy more popular? Can a more popular philosophy still retain its serious purpose? How can such a popular philosophy secure for itself a future in a world that will be increasingly ruled by the two gods of philistinism and technocracy: **money and technology**?

this is so empowering!

THE CHARGE OF SEXISM

★ As well as the charge of academic irrelevance and sterility, there is another aspect of philosophy that brings it into disrepute. It is probably obvious to you that almost all the philosophers mentioned in the story were men.

do you think men need to do away with philosophy?

just play the game

Second Sex

The existentialist **Simone de Beauvoir** famously proclaimed that women were always looked upon as the "second sex."

A RATIONAL DISPUTE

★ Surely, you might say—and if you did, you would be in good company—there must be something wrong with any approach to understanding the world that fails to take account of the answers to the fundamental questions of everyday life provided by over half the human race: **women**.

★ This may cause some disquieting questions in the mind of the philosopher. IS PHILOSOPHY INHERENTLY SEXIST? PERHAPS RACIST TOO? **Is not philosophy the obscure speculative fantasies of dead white European men?**

★ *Does this mean doing away with philosophy and reconstructing something else in its place?* Many contemporary feminists would say yes. However, most of these feminists chide philosophy for being a hotbed of male **rationalism**, a way of thinking that emphasizes our separation from objects, others, and even parts of our very selves. **Rationalism values logic and mathematics as the highest forms of thought, and so it tends to favor technique and proof over imagination and creativity.** Many feminists claim that this MASCULINIST RATIONALISM is a way of thinking and speaking (a discourse) that empowers men and DISEMPOWERS WOMEN, and as such it needs to be contested root and branch.

IN DEFENSE OF PHILOSOPHY

The French feminist "philosopher" **Luce Irigaray** (1932–) can be read as trying to construct a more vital and "elemental" philosophy that is not dissimilar to pre-Socratic philosophy.

THE PRE-SOCRATICS

★ However, it would be a mistake to accuse the pre-Socratics of this kind of thinking. Their philosophies were **"pre-rational"** and driven by a prelinguistic sense of speculative wonder. With such PRE-PLATONIC PHILOSOPHY, no clear distinction can be made between **reason** and **imagination. Most feminist criticisms of philosophy are really directed against technocratic, not philosophical, ways of thinking.**

★ For the pre-Socratics, philosophy was essentially a creative activity that was about as far removed from logic and analysis as anyone could imagine. Although traditional philosophers see the pre-Socratics as being like amateur scientists, recent research has showed that they were more like itinerant teachers who wanted to open the mind to the strange mysteries of the cosmos.

philosophy is the obscure speculative fantasy of dead white European men

PHILOSOPHERS AT PLAY

★ As the French philosopher Gilles Deleuze (1925-95) argued, philosophy at its most useful is about the creation of concepts, not for the purpose of theory-building, but for their own sake. Hence philosophy is an essentially playful exercise, a free play of thinking. This version of philosophy is clearly an improvement on the current definitions provided by technocrats and philistines. However, we might be able to extract a more serious point from Deleuze's claim. To teach people to philosophize is to teach them the art of concept creation—ways of thinking about ourselves and the world that can be both playful and instructive.

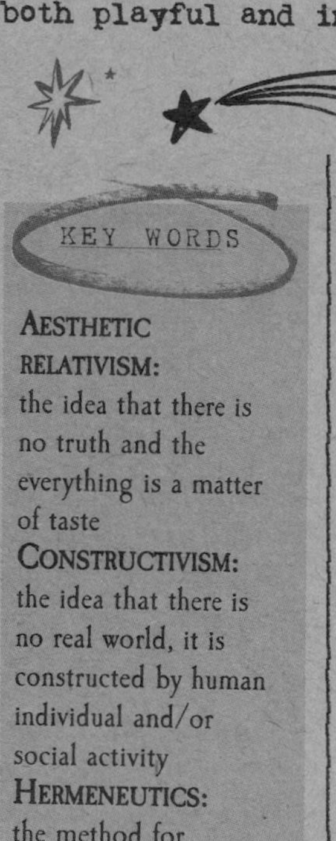

KEY WORDS

AESTHETIC RELATIVISM: the idea that there is no truth and the everything is a matter of taste

CONSTRUCTIVISM: the idea that there is no real world, it is constructed by human individual and/or social activity

HERMENEUTICS: the method for making sense of unfamiliar things (especially ancient texts)

philosophers at play

A SPIRITUAL ROLE

★ **If philosophy can teach people to construct concepts**, then it can teach people to **recreate a world** for themselves where they can view both themselves and the wider world as having a new and deeper kind of significance. This is to view philosophy as providing answers to modern nihilism and existential despair, a very Nietzschean suggestion in that it would place philosophy in the role of a kind of "spiritual instructor" in a postreligious, postmetaphysical age.

philosophy can be a modern guru

OUR WORLD

* However, Nietzsche's ideas on their own lead to the intellectual dead-end of aesthetic relativism, a philosophical view that denies the reality of any "world in common" and champions the harsh values of art over those of ethics. To avoid this easy constructivism in philosophy we need to assert, with Heidegger, that we all "always already" exist in the "real" world of others and other objects. Instead of us asking questions of this world, this world asks **questions of us**. We need to listen to the world in new ways and hear the fundamental questions that it asks of us. This ability to "listen" philosophically forms part of our basic sense of **concern** for the world we live in. So philosophy is not simply about the art of concept creation, it should be about helping people to listen to themselves and others in new and more sensitive ways.

* This idea is perhaps best captured by the idea of the German philosopher Hans Georg Gadamer that philosophy should be **hermeneutic**; it should not be about method but about teaching people how to engage in a dialogue with the world around them.

AN OPEN MIND

The big questions of everyday life cannot be answered unless we approach them in a pre-Socratic spirit: with an open mind, a sensitive imagination, and a willingness to listen. As long as these questions are asked in this way, they will never appear irrelevant or silly.

philosophy has the answers

how's the construction going, Jim?

Ask the question

Contemporary philosophy needs to regain its confidence in its own distinctive way of asking questions. Only then will philosophers be able to address themselves to the concerns that face people at the end of the second millennium.

Philosophy, the goddess of truth and wonder

OUR IMAGINATION

*** So, according to this philosophy (let's call it ethical constructivism) human existence has wonder at its very core, and it is our very "openness" to the world that makes us both free to create in it and be responsible for our creations at the same time.**

CREATIVE SPACE

* This openness is a space for the exercise of the FREE IMAGINATION where we can represent the world to ourselves as we wish. *At the same time it is the space where the world asks us what our constructions are for and why we have chosen to represent the world as we have.*

* So real life philosophical thought derives from an opening, the "STILL CENTER" of human existence, the point where freedom meets responsibility, rationality meets imagination, and self meets other. This point is the source of all that is **humanly significant**. Thus one can make an even stronger claim about the significance of philosophy than **Socrates** did: *the unexamined life is not only not worth living, it isn't even a life. It is the way of nonlife: an ossified fossil of existence that only philosophy can cure.*

why have we chosen to represent the world in the way we have?

philosophy can stop our lives from becoming fossilized

UNWRAP THE MUMMY

Nietzsche thought that academic philosophers had turned philosophy into a "mummy" and hence they were more like Egyptologists than honest seekers of the truth. I hope this book has shown that if we unwrap this mummy, the ancient jewel of philosophy is still there.

ESSENTIAL PHILOSOPHY

★ **Parmenides** said *only philosophy can lead us into the true light of being.* This might seem so much hogwash to those who sympathize with the philistines. **But without wonder, the world can only appear in the negative, and without some idea of truth, then all our ideas are just a babble of pointless opinions.** If the PHILOSOPHICAL GODDESS is the guardian of both of these, then she keeps safe two of the most precious ideas that we have.

it's a wonderful life

A

B

C

D

E

F

G

*H

*I

*J

*K

*L

*M

*N

*P